Inhalt

Vorwort
Liste der Arbeitsaufträge

Hinweise, Tipps und Übungsaufgaben zu den Kompetenzbereichen

1	Kompetenzbereich: Listening	1
1.1	Strategien zum Kompetenzbereich „Listening"	1
1.2	Häufige Aufgabenstellungen zum Kompetenzbereich „Listening"	3
1.3	Übungsaufgaben zum Kompetenzbereich „Listening"	4
	Listening Test 1: Mrs Forsyth-Brown	4
	Listening Test 2: How may I help you, madam?	6
	Listening Test 3: Waves on the water	8
	Listening Test 4: You need more than a flashy new moped	11
	Listening Test 5: Everyone needs a friend	13
2	Kompetenzbereich: Reading	15
2.1	Strategien zum Kompetenzbereich „Reading"	15
2.2	Häufige Aufgabenstellungen zum Kompetenzbereich „Reading"	16
2.3	Übungsaufgaben zum Kompetenzbereich „Reading"	17
	Reading Test 1: A holiday on the water	17
	Reading Test 2: Earning, working, learning	22
	Reading Test 3: The hunters and the hunted: who's for dinner?	25
	Reading Test 4: An interview	29
	Reading Test 5: Charities	33
	Reading Test 6: The Royal Theatre	37
	Reading Test 7: Scene2	41
	Reading Test 8: The Australian Aborigines	45
3	Kompetenzbereich: Sprechen (English in use)	49
3.1	Strategien zum Kompetenzbereich „Sprechen" (English in use)	49
3.2	Häufige Aufgabenstellungen zum Kompetenzbereich „Sprechen" (English in use)	52
3.3	Hilfreiche Wendungen zum Kompetenzbereich „Sprechen" (English in use)	53
3.4	Übungsaufgaben zum Kompetenzbereich „Sprechen" (English in use)	54
4	Kompetenzbereich: Writing	64
4.1	Strategien zum Kompetenzbereich „Writing"	64
4.2	Hilfreiche Wendungen zum Kompetenzbereich „Writing"	66

Fortsetzung siehe nächste Seite

Inhalt

4.3 Häufige Aufgabenstellungen zum Kompetenzbereich „Writing" 69
4.4 Übungsaufgaben zum Kompetenzbereich „Writing" 70

Anhang: Kurzgrammatik

1	Adverbien – *adverbs*	83
2	Bedingungssätze – *if-clauses*	84
3	Fürwörter – *pronouns*	86
4	Grundform – *infinitive*	87
5	Indirekte Rede – *reported speech*	87
6	Modale Hilfsverben – *modal auxiliaries*	89
7	Konjunktionen – *conjunctions*	90
8	Partizipien – *participles*	91
9	Passiv – *passive voice*	93
10	Präpositionen – *prepositions*	94
11	Relativsätze – *relative clauses*	97
12	Steigerung und Vergleich – *comparisons*	98
13	Wortstellung – *word order*	99
14	Zeiten – *tenses*	100

Original-Aufgaben der Abschlussprüfung an Realschulen in Hamburg

Abschlussprüfung 2005 2005-1
    Leseverstehen 2005-1
    Textproduktion 2005-5
    Sprechen (English in use) 2005-7

Abschlussprüfung 2006 2006-1
    Hörverstehen 2006-1
    Leseverstehen 2006-3
    Textproduktion 2006-6
    Sprechen (English in use) 2006-8

Autoren: Paul Jenkinson (Übungsaufgaben, Lösung des Jahrgangs 2005)
             Michael Haseleu (Lösung des Jahrgangs 2006)

Vorwort

Liebe Schülerin, lieber Schüler,

Prüfungen sind manchmal mit Angst verbunden: Angst vor Wissenslücken, vor der eigenen Schusseligkeit oder vor der ungewohnten Situation. Die meisten dieser Ängste lassen sich bekämpfen, indem du dich langfristig und nachhaltig auf deine Prüfungen vorbereitest.

Mit dem vorliegenden Buch kannst du dich schon **ab der 9. Klasse gezielt** mit den **verschiedenen Kompetenzbereichen der englischen Sprache** vertraut machen und selbstständig und effektiv auf **die zentral gestellte Abschlussprüfung** an der Realschule im Fach Englisch hinarbeiten.

- Jedes Kapitel widmet sich einem **Kompetenzbereich**. In den ersten Abschnitten erfährst du jeweils, welche Anforderungen auf dich zukommen können und wie du dich am besten darauf vorbereitest.
- Anhand der **Übungen** kannst du trainieren, wie man mit möglichen Aufgabenstellungen aus den verschiedenen Fertigkeitsbereichen umgeht und wie man sie erfolgreich löst.
- Die beiliegende **Audio-CD** enthält alle Hörverstehenstexte. Außerdem findest du die Texte abgedruckt im Lösungsteil. Versuche, die entsprechenden Fragen nur durch Zuhören (und nicht durch Nachschlagen!) zu beantworten.
- Eine Auswahl **hilfreicher Wendungen**, die dir sicherlich in den unterschiedlichsten Bereichen nützlich sein werden, erleichtert dir das selbstständige Verfassen kleiner wie größerer Texte sowie die Vorbereitung auf den Kompetenzbereich Sprechen (English in use).
- In der **Kurzgrammatik** werden alle wichtigen grammatischen Themen knapp erläutert und an Beispielsätzen veranschaulicht. Hier kannst du dich informieren, wenn du in der Grammatik einmal unsicher sein solltest.
- Das beiliegende **Lösungsheft** enthält ausführliche Lösungsvorschläge mit vielen wertvollen Hinweisen und Tipps zum Lösen der Aufgaben.
- Am Ende des Buches findest du die **Original-Aufgaben der Abschlussprüfungen 2005 und 2006**. Anhand dieser Aufgaben und der zugehörigen Lösungsvorschläge kannst du deine Kenntnisse sozusagen „unter Prüfungsbedingungen" testen.

Wir wünschen dir viel Spaß beim Üben und viel Erfolg in der Prüfung!

Liste der Arbeitsaufträge

Die in den zentralen gestellten Aufgaben verwendeten Arbeitsaufträge werden hier erklärt und mit Beispielen veranschaulicht. Dies sind die von der Hamburger Behörde für Bildung und Sport festgelegten Arbeitsaufträge, die Teil deiner Prüfung sein können.

Arbeitsaufträge	Erklärung Ziel der Anweisung	Beispiele
choose	Choose/Pick one or more alternatives from a number of different possibilities.	Choose the correct tense of the verb to fit the gap. → siehe 2005 Aufgabe 3.1
collect	Collect/Put together certain aspects or information.	Collect reasons for bullying in schools.
comment on	Give your own opinion about something.	Comment on Susan's behaviour towards her parents.
complete/finish	Complete/finish something e. g. a short story or a dialogue making sure you understand the context. Use your own words.	Finish the dialogue bearing in mind the story so far. Complete the following statements. Finish the sentences according to the text.
describe	Say what someone or something is like.	Describe the special effects in a film you have seen.
explain	Give reasons for something or explain a word.	Explain why Susan ran away from home. Explain the following words from the text.
find words	Find suitable words for a particular context.	Find the word which is the odd man out. Find 10 words that describe leisure time activities. → siehe 2005 Aufgabe 3.2, 2006 Aufgabe 3.2
fill in	Write a word or phrase in a grid or a gap in order to show that you understand certain information or to complete sentences.	Fill in the grid with information about John (name, age, hobby etc.) while listening to the interview with him. Fill in the missing information in the numbered spaces.
make a mind map	Collect words and expressions which have something to do with a particular theme or word-field.	Make a mind map for the word-field food (vegetable, milk products, fruit …)
mark	Underline or highlight certain parts of a text.	Mark the parts of the text which refer to …
match	Connect two or more things (e. g. with a line) to show you understand the meaning e. g. words and their definitions.	Match the correct definitions to the words.
number	Number things to show that you understand the correct order.	Number the pictures in the correct order.
put the words in the correct order	… to show that you can construct a sentence correctly.	
take notes/ note down	Write down keywords and sentences in order to show that you understand the main points in a text.	Read the text and take notes on Jim's hobbies. Note down the most important information in the text.

Liste der Arbeitsaufträge

tick	Put a tick (✓) to show if a statement is correct or not, or to choose the correct one from two or more (multiple choice).	Tick the correct sentences. Tick *right (true)/wrong (false)* or *not in the text*. → siehe 2005 Aufgabe 1.1, 1.2, 2006 Aufgabe 1.1, 1.2, 1.3, 3.1
underline	Draw a line under a word or a sentence.	Underline the correct ending of each sentence. Underline the mistakes.
write a letter	Write an informal letter using certain keywords (e. g. about something you experienced) or write a formal letter for a specific purpose (e. g. to complain about something).	Write a letter of application for a job. Write a postcard about your holidays. → siehe 2005 Aufgabe 2, 2006 Aufgabe 2
write/make notes	Write down ideas (in preparation for a piece of writing).	Write/make notes on how the story might end.

Hinweise, Tipps und Übungsaufgaben zu den Kompetenzbereichen

1 Kompetenzbereich: Listening

Hörverstehenstexte und die dazugehörigen Aufgabenstellungen können sehr unterschiedlich sein. Die Texte, die du im Rahmen von Abschlussprüfungen zu hören bekommst, spiegeln meist **reale Sprechsituationen** wider, d. h. man kann solche oder ähnliche Texte im „wirklichen Leben" hören. Die Inhalte der Texte können von der Begrüßungsansprache eines Flugkapitäns über die Lautsprecheransagen an einem Bahnhof oder die Kommentierung eines Fußballspiels bis hin zu Gesprächen zwischen mehreren Personen reichen. Bei Hörtexten kann es sich aber auch um kleine Geschichten oder Erzählungen zu den unterschiedlichsten Themen handeln.

Genauso vielfältig wie die verschiedenen Arten von Hörtexten können auch die Aufgabenstellungen ausfallen. In diesem Kapitel werden dir die häufigsten Textarten und Aufgabenstellungen zum Bereich „Listening" vorgestellt.

1.1 Strategien zum Kompetenzbereich „Listening"

Vorgehen in der Abschlussprüfung

In der Abschlussprüfung hörst du den **Hörverstehenstext** in der Regel **zweimal**. Er wird dir von einer CD vorgespielt.

Arbeitsschritt 1

Vor dem ersten Vorspielen des Textes hast du meist etwas Zeit, in der du dir die **Aufgabenstellungen** auf dem Arbeitsblatt **ansehen** darfst. Lies dabei die Aufgabenstellungen ganz sorgfältig durch und überlege genau, auf welche Kerninformationen es in den Aufgaben ankommt. Auf sie musst du beim Hören besonders achten. Zu den Aufgaben, die du nach dem ersten Hören bereits beantworten kannst, kannst du gleich die **richtige Lösung aufschreiben**.

Arbeitsschritt 2

Beim zweiten Hördurchgang kannst du zum einen deine Antworten noch einmal überprüfen und zum anderen die übrigen noch verbleibenden Aufgaben beantworten. Da du vor dem ersten Hören die Arbeitsaufträge lesen konntest, weißt du, welche **Detailinformationen** gefragt sind. Solche Detailinformationen können beispielsweise Adressen sein oder es werden Eigennamen buchstabiert, die du zur Lösung einer Aufgabe exakt aufschreiben musst. In solchen Fällen lohnt es sich, während des Hörens **Notizen** zu machen.

Arbeitsschritt 3

Nach dem zweiten Hören hast du in der Regel genügend Zeit, um jede Aufgabe auf deinem Arbeitsblatt noch einmal gründlich durchzulesen und entsprechend zu überprüfen. Hast du nach dem ersten Hören bereits einige Aufgaben beantwortet, so überprüfe sie jetzt noch einmal auf ihre Richtigkeit. Bei Detailinformationen, die innerhalb von einzelnen Aufgaben gefragt sind, solltest du zur Beantwortung deine Notizen heranziehen und die Antworten auf das Aufgabenblatt übertragen.

Einen Punkt solltest du immer beachten: Die Fragen folgen in der Regel dem Textverlauf, d. h. wenn du die Lösung zu einer der mittleren Fragen nicht weißt, dann passe beim zweiten Hören besonders gut in der Mitte des Textes auf.

TIPP

- Vor dem ersten Hören: Worum geht es im Text? Lies die Aufgabenstellungen genau durch.
- Nach dem ersten Hören: Trage die Lösungen zu den Aufgaben ein, die du schon beantworten kannst. Welche Informationen fehlen dir noch?
- Mache dir bei umfangreicheren Aufgabenstellungen Notizen über Details, die du für die Beantwortung von Fragen brauchst.
- Nach dem zweiten Hören: Löse die restlichen Aufgaben. Überprüfe noch einmal die Aufgaben, die du nach dem ersten Hören bereits gelöst hast.

Vorgehen beim Üben

Zu Übungszwecken kannst du dir den Hörverstehenstext ruhig so oft anhören, wie du möchtest. Lies ihn aber nicht durch! Versuche, die Arbeitsaufträge nur durch Zuhören zu beantworten. Nur wenn du überhaupt nicht auf die richtige Lösung kommst, solltest du den Hörverstehenstext im Lösungsteil dieses Buches lesen. Bei der Bearbeitung der Hörverstehensaufgaben in diesem Buch solltest du wie folgt vorgehen:

▶ Lies die Aufgabenstellungen genau durch. Hast du sie alle verstanden? Kläre unbekannte Wörter mithilfe eines Wörterbuches.

▶ Höre dir den entsprechenden Text einmal an, sodass du weißt, worum es darin geht.

▶ Höre dir den Text noch einmal an. Diesen Schritt kannst du so oft wiederholen, wie es für dich hilfreich ist.

▶ Höre dir den Text an und versuche dabei, die Aufgaben zu lösen.

▶ Wenn du alle Aufgaben bearbeitet hast, solltest du die Richtigkeit deiner Lösungen überprüfen, indem du dir den Text ein weiteres Mal anhörst.

▶ Anschließend überprüfst du deine Antworten anhand der Lösungen am Ende des Buches. Wenn du viele Fehler gemacht hast, dann überlege genau, wie sie zustande gekommen sind. Hast du den Hörtext nicht genau verstanden? Hast du die Fragestellung falsch verstanden? Lies gegebenenfalls den Hörverstehenstext durch und wiederhole die gesamte Aufgabe in ein paar Wochen.

▶ Versuche, mit der Bearbeitung jeder weiteren Hörverstehensaufgabe in diesem Buch die Zahl der Hörsequenzen zu reduzieren, bis du bei der in der Prüfung üblichen Anzahl angelangt bist. In der Prüfung werden die Texte nur zweimal vorgespielt.

1.2 Häufige Aufgabenstellungen zum Kompetenzbereich „Listening"

Right or wrong or not in the text

Diesen Aufgabentyp kennst du sicher schon lange aus dem Unterricht. Du sollst jeweils entscheiden, ob eine Aussage richtig oder falsch ist. Meist weicht dabei die Formulierung der Aussage in der Aufgabenstellung etwas von der im Text ab. Manchmal wird auch als dritte Auswahlmöglichkeit „not in the text" vorgegeben. In diesem Fall kann es also sein, dass Aussagen vorgegeben werden, die nichts mit dem Hörtext zu tun haben.

Listening text: "It was ten minutes to the bus station." right ✓ wrong ☐ — *Beispiel*
Statement: It didn't take longer than a few minutes to go to the bus station.

Multiple choice

Auch dieser Aufgabentyp ist dir bestimmt schon vertraut. Dir wird eine Frage mit mehreren möglichen Antworten vorgegeben und du musst entscheiden, welche Antwort am besten zum Inhalt des Textes passt. Auch hier wird die Formulierung in der Aufgabenstellung variiert.

Listening text: "I'm sorry I'm late. The bus didn't come so I had to walk home and get my bike." — *Beispiel*
Question: Why was the man late?
☐ the bus was late and he cycled
☐ he walked
✓ there was no bus

Answering in short expressions / single word answers

Hier werden dir Fragen gestellt, die du mit ein oder zwei Stichwörtern beantworten kannst. Du musst keine vollständigen Sätze schreiben.

Listening text: "The man took his umbrella because it was raining but it was too windy for him to use it." — *Beispiel*
Question: Why didn't the man use his umbrella?
Answer: _It was too windy._

Summary

Immer wieder können dir auch Aufgabenstellungen begegnen, in denen dir „guided notes" – also etwa ein Lückentext – vorgegeben werden. Du musst dann auf der Grundlage dessen, was du gehört hast, Lücken füllen oder Stichwörter ergänzen. Hier können dir auch Aufgaben begegnen, in denen du den englischen Text oder bestimmte Zusammenhänge aus dem englischen Text in deutscher Sprache wiedergeben musst. Diese Variante hat für dich den Vorteil, dass du keine Grammatik- oder Rechtschreibfehler in der Fremdsprache Englisch machen kannst.

1.3 Übungsaufgaben zum Kompetenzbereich „Listening"

T 1   **Listening Test 1: Mrs Forsyth-Brown**

Vokabeln

dear	– *(hier)* Liebling
darling	– *(hier)* Liebling/Schätzchen
posh (-er/-est)	– piekfein
Gap	– Markenname
homeless	– *(hier)* herumstreunend

Worksheet

1. Listen to the text and tick (✓) what is right or wrong.   right wrong
   a) Mrs Forsyth-Brown is telling her friend about her holiday. ☐ ☐
   b) Mrs Forsyth-Brown likes Max's friends. ☐ ☐
   c) Mrs Forsyth-Brown doesn't like what Max is wearing. ☐ ☐
   d) Mrs Forsyth-Brown is shocked about what she finds out. ☐ ☐
   e) Mrs Forsyth-Brown is deciding which clothes to wear. ☐ ☐

2. Which sentence describes the story the best?
   ☐ It is a story about Max and his friends.
   ☐ It is a story about a boy who finds his mother embarrassing.
   ☐ It is a story about a mother who wants her son to come home early.

3. Write simple answers to the following questions. You do not have to write complete sentences.
   For example: Question: Where were the family on holiday?
                    Answer: in Cornwall

   a) Does Max like being called 'Maximilian'?
   _____
   _____

   b) What were Max and his mother doing yesterday?
   _____
   _____

   c) Why does Mrs Forsyth-Brown want to phone Sandy's mum?
   _____
   _____

Kompetenzbereich: Listening | 5

Damit du möglichst viele Übungsmöglichkeiten hast, werden hier zusätzliche Aufgaben zum Hörtest 1 angeboten. Du kannst den Text weitere Male anhören und dabei die folgenden Aufgaben lösen.

Hinweis

4. Listen to the text and tick (✓) what is right or wrong. right wrong

   a) Mrs Forsyth-Brown and her friend are going to meet for coffee at 3.30. ☐ ☐
   b) Mrs Forsyth-Brown thinks 10 o'clock is early. ☐ ☐
   c) Max doesn't like how his mother is. ☐ ☐
   d) Max has got three very good friends. ☐ ☐
   e) James waits on the doorstep for Max. ☐ ☐
   f) Max is looking for his training shoes. ☐ ☐
   g) Mrs Forsyth-Brown likes Sandy. ☐ ☐
   h) Max is cheeky *(frech)* to his mother. ☐ ☐
   i) Mrs Forsyth-Brown decides to have blue fingernails. ☐ ☐

Additional tasks

Kompetenzbereich: Listening

T 2

Listening Test 2: How may I help you, madam?

Worksheet

1. Read each question carefully. Which answer is correct?
   a) What is the telephone number of FlyEasy?
      - [ ] 600345
      - [ ] 6200354
      - [ ] 600354

   b) Why can't Ms Lawson talk to Marie?
      - [ ] Marie doesn't work in the office anymore.
      - [ ] Marie is ill, on Friday she hurt her back.
      - [ ] Marie won't be at work again until Friday.

   c) What are the dates Ms Lawson gives?
      - [ ] 13th July to 21st July
      - [ ] 30th June to 21st July
      - [ ] 13th July to 31st July

   d) Does Ms Lawson like continental breakfasts?
      - [ ] Yes, she does.
      - [ ] No, she doesn't.
      - [ ] The answer is not in the dialogue.

   e) Why doesn't Ms Lawson need a plane reservation?
      - [ ] she doesn't like flying
      - [ ] Humphrey is happier going by car
      - [ ] there's no room for Humphrey on a plane

   f) Why does the travel agent think Ms Lawson needs a double room?
      - [ ] he thinks she wants more space
      - [ ] he thinks she is taking a friend with her
      - [ ] two people cannot share a single room

2. Tell the story to a friend. Fill in the missing words.

   Ms Lawson wanted to make a hotel _____ in Nice. The person she had talked to yesterday was not in the _____. Mike, another travel agent, asked if he could _____ her. Mike did not know that the woman was travelling with her _____ called Humphrey. He thought Humphrey was a real _____. Ms Lawson became very angry with Mike and put the _____ down.

Kompetenzbereich: Listening | 7

3. Understanding the conversation.
   Give simple answers to the following questions:

   a) What is Mike's job?

   _____
   _____

   b) How will Ms Lawson get to Nice?

   _____
   _____

   c) Why does Ms Lawson need a single room with a lot of floor space?

   _____
   _____

   d) Has Ms Lawson been to the travel agent's before or has she only phoned them?

   _____
   _____

4. Read each question carefully. Which answer is correct?   *Additional tasks*

   a) What exactly does Ms Lawson want to do?
      - [ ] She wants to book a double room.
      - [ ] She wants to book a hotel room.
      - [ ] She wants a nice holiday somewhere.

   b) Does Ms Lawson smoke?
      - [ ] Yes, she does.
      - [ ] No, she doesn't.
      - [ ] The answer is not in the dialogue.

   c) Who is Humphrey?
      - [ ] a friend
      - [ ] her brother
      - [ ] her pet

Kompetenzbereich: Listening

T 3

Listening Test 3: Waves on the water

Vokabeln
scary   – unheimlich/angsteinflößend
sleeping-bag – Schlafsack

Worksheet

1. Tick (✓) the right answer.

   a) What has Liz been doing?
      ☐ looking at the weather
      ☐ having a holiday
      ☐ watching something scary

   b) Where do you find the mist?
      ☐ in Scotland
      ☐ on the hills
      ☐ near water

   c) Which city did Liz visit?
      ☐ the Highlands
      ☐ Loch Ness
      ☐ Edinburgh

   d) Why does Liz get angry?
      ☐ because she wants Tom to think she is angry
      ☐ because Tom doesn't believe her
      ☐ because Tom teases *(hänseln)* her

   e) Where was Liz's tent?
      ☐ next to the main road
      ☐ on the opposite side of the loch to the main road
      ☐ on the water

   f) Why did Liz go to sleep?
      ☐ she was frightened
      ☐ she was cold
      ☐ she was tired

   g) What is Liz's story?
      ☐ a story to tease Tom
      ☐ about her visit to Scotland
      ☐ about her holiday

2. Listen to the whole story <u>then</u> answer the questions. You do not have to write complete sentences.

   a) What type of holiday did Liz have and where did she go?
   _____
   _____

   b) Describe the Scottish weather.
   _____
   _____

   c) Describe the Loch Ness area.
   _____
   _____

   d) What does Liz say happened?
   _____
   _____

   e) Why wasn't Liz scared?
   _____
   _____

Damit du möglichst viele Übungsmöglichkeiten hast, werden hier zusätzliche Aufgaben zum Hörtest 1 angeboten. Du kannst den Text weitere Male anhören und dabei die folgenden Aufgaben lösen.

Hinweis

3. Tick (✓) the right answer.

   Additional tasks

   a) What is the weather like in Scotland?
      - [ ] it's often sunny
      - [ ] it always rains
      - [ ] it often rains but there is usually some sunshine, too

   b) How long was Liz at Loch Ness?
      - [ ] a short time
      - [ ] a long time
      - [ ] a week

   c) Has Tom visited Loch Ness?
      - [ ] yes
      - [ ] no
      - [ ] not in the dialogue

d) Where do many of the tourists come from?
- [ ] Scotland
- [ ] Europe
- [ ] USA

e) At least how many days did Liz stay at Loch Ness?
- [ ] one
- [ ] two
- [ ] three

f) What exactly does Liz say she saw?
- [ ] big waves
- [ ] a large, dark object
- [ ] a misty morning

4. Fill in the missing words from the CD. Give the opposite that fits each sentence, too.
For example: But the weather wasn't too *good*_____.
   *bad*_____

a) I said you'd _____ and wouldn't believe me.
   _____

b) Loch Ness, the monster – _____ makes a joke about it …
   _____

c) The _____ we ever get is five miles up the road.
   _____

d) Well, Loch Ness area is in a really long, _____ valley.
   _____

e) But we were on the other side, the _____ side, camping.
   _____

f) The second _____ it started getting cold …
   _____

g) … so we lit a fire and then the mist _____.
   _____

h) I woke up _____ and looked outside.
   _____

i) _____, the water became rough and small waves came to the bank.
   _____

Kompetenzbereich: Listening | 11

Listening Test 4: You need more than a flashy new moped

T 4

Vokabeln

flashy	– auffallend/auffällig
(to) fancy	– *(hier)* gern haben
Sis' *(auch* sis'*)*	– *(slang short form)* sister
not exactly	– *(hier)* nicht gerade
(to) impress	– beeindrucken
doing (hair)	– (die Haare) (zurecht)machen
(to) fall about laughing	– sich kaputtlachen

Worksheet

1. Are the following sentences right, wrong or not in the text?
   right wrong not in the text

   a) Susie is quite busy.
   b) Pete has just bought a new moped.
   c) Susie is younger than Pete.
   d) Pete is learning to drive.
   e) Pete hasn't spoken to Jill yet.
   f) Susie thinks Jill is pretty but doesn't really like her.
   g) Pete is a romantic sort of person.
   h) Susie and Pete's mother is just coming in.
   i) Susie has had a lot of boyfriends.
   j) Susie tells Pete that the best thing about him is himself.
   k) Pete will phone Jill straight away.
   l) Susie wants to meet someone Pete knows.

2. Find the correct ending to each of the following sentences.
   a) Susie listens to Pete because she
      ☐ knows he wants to talk about something.
      ☐ thinks it's better than doing her English.
      ☐ likes him.
   b) Susie gets angry with Pete because he
      ☐ won't talk to Jill.
      ☐ won't do anything.
      ☐ is cheeky *(frech)*.
   c) Pete doesn't want to talk to Jill face to face because
      ☐ he's scared of her.
      ☐ he's embarrassed.
      ☐ she's had a lot of boyfriends.

d) Pete doesn't phone Jill because he
- [ ] can't find her mobile phone number.
- [ ] hasn't got her number.
- [ ] is too embarrassed.

e) Susie shows she likes Dave because
- [ ] she plays football.
- [ ] he's Pete's friend.
- [ ] she wants to phone him.

3. Tell the story in English using your own words. Write about 8 sentences. You can use the notes.
   - *Pete will von seiner Schwester einige Ratschläge über Mädchen.*
   - *Er mag ein Mädchen, das Jill heißt, aber er weiß nicht, was er tun soll.*
   - *Seine Schwester Susie sagt ihm, er solle Jill fragen, ob sie in einen Film gehen wolle.*
   - *Pete findet es zu peinlich, das zu tun.*
   - *Seine Schwester schlägt vor, dass er Jill anruft.*
   - *Pete hat Jills Telefonnummer nicht.*
   - *Aber Susie sagt ihm, er solle Jills Freundin danach fragen.*
   - *Susie bittet Pete dann um die Telefonnummer eines Jungen, den sie mag.*

Kompetenzbereich: Listening 13

Listening Test 5: Everyone needs a friend

T 5

1. Tick (✓) the right answer.

	right	wrong	not in the text
a) Jenny believes what Jack says.	☐	☐	☐
b) Jack is reading alone.	☐	☐	☐
c) Jack wants Jenny to go away.	☐	☐	☐
d) Jack lives alone.	☐	☐	☐
e) At first, Jack doesn't want to tell Jenny anything.	☐	☐	☐
f) Jenny gets Jack and herself something to eat.	☐	☐	☐
g) Jenny's family also live far away.	☐	☐	☐
h) Jenny drives a nice car.	☐	☐	☐
i) Jenny offers to pay the train fare.	☐	☐	☐

   Worksheet

2. Answer the following questions. You do not have to write complete sentences.

   a) Why does Jenny go and talk to Jack?
   _____

   b) What is Jack's problem?
   _____

   c) What does Jenny offer to do?
   _____

   d) What eventually happens?
   _____

Damit du möglichst viele Übungsmöglichkeiten hast, werden hier zusätzliche Aufgaben zum Hörtest 5 angeboten. Du kannst den Text weitere Male anhören und dabei die folgenden Aufgaben bearbeiten.

Hinweis

3. Tick (✓) the correct answer.

	right	wrong
a) It's late in the evening.	☐	☐
b) Jenny thinks no one can help Jack.	☐	☐
c) Jack's sister lives by herself.	☐	☐
d) Jack is poor.	☐	☐
e) Jenny thinks Jack is terrible.	☐	☐
f) Jenny will drive Jack from the café to the station.	☐	☐
g) Jack and Jenny aren't friends.	☐	☐
h) Jenny thinks that helping people is normal.	☐	☐
i) Jenny asks someone to take over her work for a short time.	☐	☐

   Additional tasks

4. Tell a friend the story in English in <u>less than ten</u> sentences. Here are some German words to help you know what to write about:

traurig / fragt ihn / was ist los / Schwester / Krankenhaus / besuchen / kein Geld / zahlen / Koffer packen / abholen / zum Busbahnhof mitnehmen

2 Kompetenzbereich: Reading

Es gibt viele verschiedene Arten von Lesetexten. Ebenso vielfältig können die Aufgabenstellungen dazu sein. Die Textsorten und Aufgabenstellungen, die am häufigsten in Abschlussprüfungen vorkommen, werden dir hier vorgestellt.

2.1 Strategien zum Kompetenzbereich „Reading"

Ganz gleich, welche Art von Lesetext oder welche Art von Aufgabenstellung du bearbeiten musst, die Vorgehensweise ist dabei immer dieselbe.

Zunächst einmal ist es sinnvoll, den Text an sich ganz genau zu betrachten. Manchmal kannst du bereits am **Layout**, d. h. an der Gestaltung des Textes erkennen, um welche Textsorte es geht. Wenn du weißt, ob der dir vorliegende Text eine Werbeanzeige, ein Zeitungsartikel oder ein Interview ist, dann bist du schon einen Schritt weiter. *(Arbeitsschritt 1)*

Als Nächstes solltest du den Text **genau lesen**. Lies ihn ruhig mehrmals durch. Jedes Mal findest du weitere Details, die dir vorher entgangen sind.
Unbekannte Wörter solltest du **im Wörterbuch nachschlagen**. Achte aber darauf, dass du nicht zu viele Wörter nachschaust, denn das kostet im Unterricht, bei den Hausaufgaben, bei der Klassenarbeit und auch in der Prüfung wertvolle Zeit. Manche Wörter kannst du außerdem ganz leicht aus dem **Sinnzusammenhang erschließen**.
Ganz entscheidend ist, dass du dir bei diesem Arbeitsschritt einen guten Überblick über den Inhalt deines Textes verschaffst. *(Arbeitsschritt 2)*

Nun solltest du die **Aufgabenstellungen genau lesen**, damit du weißt, unter welchen Aspekten du den Text bearbeiten sollst. Wenn du nun den Lesetext ein letztes Mal liest, kannst du dabei ganz gezielt wichtige **Schlüsselwörter bzw. Textpassagen markieren** (z. B. farbig oder mit Symbolen), damit du sie bei der Bearbeitung der Aufgaben schnell wieder findest. *(Arbeitsschritt 3)*

Nun bist du für die Beantwortung der Aufgaben gut gerüstet!

TIPP
- Schaue dir den Lesetext genau an. Kannst du vom „Layout" auf die Textsorte schließen?
- Lies den Text mehrmals genau durch. Schlage unbekannte Wörter im Wörterbuch nach. Verschaffe dir so einen guten Überblick über den Inhalt des Textes.
- Lies die Aufgabenstellungen genau. Markiere beim nochmaligen Lesen des Textes wichtige Textaussagen im Hinblick auf die Aufgabenstellungen.

2.2 Häufige Aufgabenstellungen zum Kompetenzbereich „Reading"

Right or wrong or not in the text

Oft wird dir eine Aussage vorgelegt und du musst entscheiden, ob sie richtig ist oder nicht. Manchmal ist die Frage etwas anders ausgedrückt als der entsprechende Satz im Text. Vielfach wird auch eine dritte Auswahlmöglichkeit, nämlich „not in the text", angeboten. In diesem Fall kann es also sein, dass Aussagen vorgegeben werden, die so nicht im Lesetext stehen.

Beispiel

Text: The nights were noisy and Peter found it difficult to go to sleep. He woke up at 5.30 a.m. every day.
Statement: Peter was tired after his holiday.   right ✓   wrong ☐

Wenn du dich nicht entscheiden kannst, welche Antwort richtig ist, dann stelle dir selbst die Frage.

Beispiel

War Peter nach seinen Ferien müde? War Peter nach seinen Ferien <u>nicht</u> müde?

Dieses Buch soll dir beim Üben helfen, rate also nicht einfach. Wenn du die Antwort nicht weißt, dann lass eine Lücke. Markiere die Fragen, bei denen du dir nicht sicher bist. Schaue im Lösungsteil erst dann nach, wenn du die ganze Übung bearbeitet hast, und versuche herauszufinden, warum die Antwort so und nicht anders lauten musste.

Multiple choice

Du bekommst Fragen mit verschiedenen Antworten. Lies die Fragen und die möglichen Antworten genau. Beachte aber, dass sie häufig anders formuliert sind als im Text. Versuche nun, die Antwort herauszufinden, die am besten zum Text passt. Wenn du dir unsicher bist, dann versuche es andersherum: Suche zuerst die Antworten, die falsch sind. Dann findest du vielleicht die richtige Antwort leichter. Die Reihenfolge der Fragen entspricht normalerweise dem Textaufbau, sodass du abschätzen kannst, wo im Text die Antwort steht.

Beispiel

Text: I like doing lots of things but have <u>no real hobbies</u>. I like to go to pop concerts if anyone good is playing. Sometimes I run or sometimes we go skiing.
Question: Does John have any hobbies?

✓ No, he doesn't.
☐ He and his girlfriend do a lot of sport.
☐ Running.

Labelling/ordering information

Bei diesem Aufgabentyp werden dir häufig mehrere kurze Texte vorgelegt, die du anderen Textabschnitten oder Bildern sinnvoll zuordnen musst. Auch hierbei wird überprüft, ob du englische Lesetexte verstehen kannst. Diese Art von Aufgabenstellung sowie „Multiple choice"-Aufgaben haben den Vorteil, dass du z. B. durch Rechtschreibfehler keine Punkte verlierst.

Matching sentences

Manchmal wirst du auch auf „Matching"-Aufgaben stoßen. Hier werden dir verschiedene Satzanfänge vorgegeben, die du einer Reihe von Satzenden zuordnen musst. Inhaltlich beziehen sich die Satzanfänge und Satzenden natürlich auf den Lesetext, d. h. wenn du dir unsicher bist, kannst du im Text nachlesen.

1 Mary likes …   a … when she was only 5 years old.
2 Her parents got divorced …   b … she began playing soccer.
3 When she was eleven years old …   c … Tom and his brother very much.

Beispiel

1	2	3
c	a	b

Questions on the text

Manchmal kannst du zur Beantwortung der Fragen Formulierungen aus dem Lesetext übernehmen, manchmal musst du deine Antworten aber auch ganz eigenständig formulieren. Lies die Fragen genau und suche die Antworten im Text.

Text: Jenny gets out of bed early, usually around 6.00 a.m.
Question: What <u>time</u> does Jenny get out of bed?
Answer: Jenny usually gets out of bed around 6.00 a.m.

Beispiel

Englische Fragen mit deutschen Antworten

Manchmal werden dir Arbeitsaufträge gegeben, zu denen du die Antworten im Lesetext finden und dann in gutem Deutsch aufschreiben musst. Wenn du die Lesetexte meist verstehst, im Englischen aber nicht ganz so flüssig formulieren kannst oder viele Rechtschreib- oder Grammatikfehler machst, kannst du bei diesen Aufgabentypen die volle Punktzahl erreichen.

Headings

Manchmal wirst du Überschriften für Abschnitte eines Textes finden müssen. Der Lesetext ist in Abschnitte unterteilt und dir sind mögliche Überschriften vorgegeben. Du musst dann die richtige Überschrift dem jeweiligen Textteil zuordnen.

2.3 Übungsaufgaben zum Kompetenzbereich „Reading"

Reading Test 1: A holiday on the water

Ein Freund gibt dir einen Brief und drei Fotografien. Die Fotografien stehen mit dem Brief in Zusammenhang. Lies den Brief sorgfältig und versuche die unbekannten Ausdrücke aus dem Sinnzusammenhang zu erschließen. Du musst aber nicht alle Wörter verstehen, um die wesentlichen Aussagen des Textes erfassen zu können.

Hinweise

Hi there,

I've just had a really great holiday with my parents. Normally I don't go on holiday with them but they decided that they wanted a different type of holiday this year. So they looked through a lot of brochures and then decided on a holiday on a boat. In England there are many different types of boat that you can hire. You can hire a sailing boat which is no fun on small rivers or if there is no wind and you have to do a lot of work all the time sailing it. You can also hire a canal boat. These are sometimes called narrow boats because they are long and thin. The last type of boat is one specially made for having holidays on. I've sent you a picture of ours and the others, too.

On our boat there were three bedrooms, a kitchen and a large sitting and eating area where you could slide the roof back – it was like having a sports car! Of course, there was also a toilet and a shower but they were small. The boat was very easy to control. Everyone had to have a short lesson first on how to control the boat; that was funny because no one had been on a boat before. But it was very easy to learn to sail it; that's funny, too, even though it has a motor you still sail it, not drive it. A week on a boat sounds boring but it wasn't. It was a lot of fun. We could stop anywhere we wanted to. Sometimes we stopped in the middle of the countryside or by small towns to buy groceries and one day we even stopped in a big city. Norwich was really nice and we visited all the sights there. But usually we just woke up, had breakfast and then went further along the river. We were in the Norfolk Broads which is an area full of rivers and small lakes, called broads, that were made by monks a long time ago. Surprisingly, there's a lot to do there, too. You can even try catching fish from your boat for your dinner!

You have to stop at night when it is getting dark, so no other boats go past you. But the hardest thing to do is to go to sleep on the boat since it is always moving up and down in the water, of course, and the countryside is really, really dark; there're no streetlights. But I discovered the countryside isn't very quiet. Every morning I was woken up by the birds or the cows or a tractor or something else at 5.30 a.m. I was really tired after my holiday!

Why I'm telling you all this is that I'd love to go again but my parents don't want to. Would you like to come with me in the summer holidays? I remember you saying that school finishes then. It's not too expensive, about £ 200 each, but I know you also need to travel from Germany. Let me know if you are interested. Maybe your parents will pay – you can always tell them it's good for your English, then I'm sure they'll want you to go! I hope you'll let me know soon. I can send you more pictures, if you want.

Have fun,
Sam

Kompetenzbereich: Reading | 19

A B C

Fotos

1. Right or wrong? Tick (✓) the correct answer.　　　　　　　right　wrong

   a) Sam enjoyed the holiday.　　　　　　　　　　　　　　□　□
   b) Sam's parents bought a boat.　　　　　　　　　　　　□　□
   c) The boat was very small.　　　　　　　　　　　　　　□　□
   d) Sam was bored on the boat.　　　　　　　　　　　　　□　□
   e) It is forbidden to sail at night.　　　　　　　　　　　　□　□
   f) Sam found the countryside noisy.　　　　　　　　　　□　□
   g) Sam does not want to go again.　　　　　　　　　　　□　□
   h) Sam took many photographs on holiday.　　　　　　□　□

Worksheet

2. Look at Sam's photographs and read the first paragraph carefully.

   a) Which is the boat Sam and his family used? Mark with a cross.

   | A | B | C |

   b) Name the type of boat in each photograph.
      Photograph A _____
      Photograph B _____
      Photograph C _____

   c) What is the area called where Sam and his family were on holiday and where exactly was the boat at the time the photograph was taken? Answer in full sentences.
      _____
      _____
      _____

3. Answer the following questions in full sentences. You may use the words from the text in your answers.

   a) Does Sam's family always go on holiday together?
      _____
      _____

b) Why did Sam's parents choose this type of holiday?

c) Why didn't Sam want a holiday on a sailing boat?

d) Before the family could use the boat what did they have to do?

e) Which city did they stop at and why?

f) What are the Norfolk Broads?

4. Answer the following questions in full sentences imagining that you received the letter. Try to use more of your own words this time and not just the ones from the letter.
   a) Why was Sam tired after his holiday?

   b) Why is Sam writing to you?

   c) Why does Sam think your parents might pay?

   d) Which month do you think Sam wants to go on holiday?

   e) How much will the holiday cost altogether?

5. Unfortunately your parents do not understand English. Explain to them some things that Sam has told you in the letter. Answer in German.
   a) Explain what type of holiday Sam had.

   b) Describe the boat to your parents.

   c) Describe the Norfolk Broads to your parents.

   d) Explain what Sam wants to know and ask if you can go.

   e) Use Sam's advice to convince your parents.

6. Your parents have some questions. Answer them in German but use the information from Sam's letter.
   a) Braucht man einen Bootsführerschein?

   b) Wo könnt ihr Lebensmittel kaufen?

   c) Wird es dir nicht langweilig werden?

   d) Ist es nachts nicht gefährlich?

   e) Wie viel wird das alles kosten?

Reading Test 2: Earning, working, learning

In Great Britain many young people have part-time jobs. These jobs used to be mainly weekend or holiday ones but today that situation is changing. As many as half of all 16-17-year-olds have some kind of job while they are still at school and as they get older that number becomes much larger. Many of these young people now work up to fifteen hours a week and not just at weekends or in their holidays.

The main areas of work are in the retail industry, for example in shops and in supermarkets. These jobs are there because many shops and supermarkets stay open longer during the week including Saturdays and also open on Sundays. Traditional part-time workers are often women with children who do not want to work late at night or away from their families at the weekends. Employers need workers for these unattractive times to work. This means, therefore, that there are a lot of jobs for young people which fit nicely around a school day.

Some people are against the idea of students in full-time education having part-time employment. They say that since these students have to work more, they spend less time on their schoolwork. In a perfect world it might be best to learn first and work later but many young people find that they need to earn money. However, the choice to work and learn is their own. No one makes them do it. The better students, though, are usually able to find a balance between work and school and can even benefit from the experience.

Many students find they develop new skills when they start work. They learn to work with other people and often have responsibilities for the first time in their lives. They discover that rules are not just for school but appear in adult life, too. If they do not do their job properly, for example, they can easily lose it. Working also provides young people with money, which makes them financially independent: how to handle your own money is an important thing to learn. Many students often add to their social life through work and they also learn to understand other people better.

There are other advantages, too. Many students who work part-time around their schoolwork have found out that they become more efficient because they have to plan what they do and use their time better. If you have a lot of time to do something, you usually don't do it until the last moment. But if you only have little time, you use it better.

Schools, of course, do not support the idea of earning and working. They complain of students handing work in late, being tired and not concentrating, spending little time on the work they do at home and, sometimes, even missing lessons. Although schools do not like their students to have part-time work, some teachers do see a positive side and can even link the experiences the students gain to topics in school. Some schools are also trying to work with employers so that their students are allowed to work less around examination times and still keep their jobs.

Although working and learning can go together, it is still not easy. Young people may take the opportunity to work but they must also understand that there are dangers in the world of work. Every week, ten young people are seriously hurt at work in Britain, some even die. Almost 40 % of 15-24-year-olds have had no health or safety training by their employers. This figure is almost certainly higher with part-time workers. Part-time workers, especially young people, are easily replaced and, therefore, they do not say, "I won't do that because it's too dangerous".

Kompetenzbereich: Reading | **23**

1. Right or wrong or not in the text? Tick (✓) the correct answer.   right / wrong / not in the text   Worksheet

   a) The part-time jobs are only weekend and holiday ones. ☐ ☐ ☐
   b) Most jobs are in shops and supermarkets. ☐ ☐ ☐
   c) There are a lot of family businesses involved. ☐ ☐ ☐
   d) Weekend workers are usually women. ☐ ☐ ☐
   e) Men get jobs a lot easier than women. ☐ ☐ ☐
   f) Most young people work part-time just for the money. ☐ ☐ ☐
   g) Working gives people responsibility. ☐ ☐ ☐
   h) In work you learn to be tolerant of other people. ☐ ☐ ☐
   i) Some students find that they are better organised when they have a job and are still at school. ☐ ☐ ☐
   j) Schools like the idea of their students working. ☐ ☐ ☐
   k) British students are allowed to miss lessons if they have to work. ☐ ☐ ☐
   l) The government helps young people to get work experience. ☐ ☐ ☐
   m) Students do not get enough information about safety at work. ☐ ☐ ☐

2. Answer the following questions using your own words as far as possible. Use <u>at least two</u> sentences in each answer.

   a) Why are there a lot of part-time jobs for students?

   _____
   _____
   _____

   b) Give three good things that young people get from working.

   _____
   _____
   _____

   c) Why are most teachers against young people having part-time jobs?

   _____
   _____
   _____

   d) How do a few schools and employers work together?

   _____
   _____
   _____

e) What hidden dangers are there for young people in work, especially with part-time jobs?
_____
_____
_____

3. Imagine that you are going to a supermarket to ask about a part-time job. The line references give you some key words or phrases from the text. Use this information to make questions about the job.

   For example: line 12: "areas of work"
   What will I have to do? / What type of work will I have to do?

   a) line 10: fifteen hours
   _____
   _____

   b) lines 16–18: longer during the week, Saturdays and Sundays
   _____
   _____

   c) line 35: money
   _____
   _____

   d) lines 80/81: work less around examinations
   _____
   _____

   e) lines 90/91: health and safety training
   _____
   _____

4. Combine the parts of the sentences. Put the correct letter below each number.

   (1) Retail work means
   (2) Most employers want young people
   (3) Many young people have part-time jobs
   (4) If you don't do your job well, you can be told
   (5) If a student has a job, he needs
   (6) When starting work you need

   a) to get money.
   b) to be well organised.
   c) to work in shops and supermarkets.
   d) to find out about the safety rules.
   e) to work at unpopular times.
   f) to leave.

(1)	(2)	(3)	(4)	(5)	(6)

Reading Test 3: The hunters and the hunted: who's for dinner?

A Australia is a very large country that is low and flat. The highest mountain is just over two thousand metres and the landscape changes a lot from good farming area to the bush, which is often hot and dry. As it has no neighbours the wildlife in the country has not changed very much for thousands of years. Australia has many interesting species; two of the best known are its large crocodiles and its kangaroos. Both were even seen in well-known films: Crocodile Dundee and Kangaroo Jack.

B Australia has two types of crocodiles, one is small and harmless but the other one is very dangerous and can grow to about seven metres. Although it is called a saltwater crocodile it lives happily in rivers. These crocodiles have no enemies and can live to a very old age; some are thought to be over 100 years old. Being 'croc-wise' is very important for Australians. 'Croc-wise' means being careful in areas where there are saltwater crocodiles, if you are not you may find yourself on the day's menu!

C Crocodiles attack by staying still in the water and waiting for their dinner to come walking by. They then spring from the water to surprise their prey and take it back with them into the water. One big meal can keep a crocodile happy for days, weeks and even months.

D There are some simple rules to obey if you are in a crocodile area so that you do not become the dish of the day. Firstly, you should stay out of the water and if you are on a boat you must not put your arms or legs into it, either. It is a good idea to stay away from riverbanks, too. If you want to camp or have a picnic in the area you should be at least fifty metres from the water and ideally two metres higher than it. Crocodiles watch and wait and they learn routines very quickly. If you are camping in an area you must not do the same thing every day near the water's edge.

E Although saltwater crocodiles are very dangerous they are protected by the Australian government. Australians like their animals very much and another protected species is the kangaroo.

F Kangaroos vary a lot in size from half a kilo to ninety kilos and there are many different types from small ones that live in trees to ones about the size of an average person. The largest ones can hop at up to 60 kmh, jump nine metres long and three metres high. They also like to live in groups, which often have about 100 kangaroos in them. They live almost everywhere in Australia since the only real thing they need is water. The Aborigines hunted the kangaroos for food and their skins, so did the early Europeans who came to Australia in 1788. Four types of kangaroos are still hunted but, although the idea of killing kangaroos and eating their meat may not seem very nice for a lot of people, Australians, in fact, look after their kangaroo population very well.

G In Australia there are about 19 million people. However, there are approximately 50 million kangaroos but only 28 million of these can be hunted. Although kangaroo meat and skins are exported the kangaroos are not kept on farms. The Australian government only allows kangaroos to be shot by official hunters. Because of the large numbers of kangaroos and because they are killed kindly no one is against it.

H Crocodiles and kangaroos may well have taken part in the movies but they are only two of the many special species that live in Australia. Many of these are just as dangerous as the man-eating crocodiles or they can be every child's dream of a cuddly toy – the koala.

Kompetenzbereich: Reading

Worksheet

1. The text has got 8 paragraphs. In the grid below there are 10 headings. Decide which is the best heading for each paragraph (A–H) and write the letter in the answer space. Two headings are wrong.

   Efficient natural hunters ☐
   Hopping, skipping and jumping ☐
   One species, many sizes ☐
   From bites to cuddles ☐
   Recognizing crocodiles ☐
   Down under ☐
   The Europeans ☐
   Protected species ☐
   Be safe ☐
   The kangaroo business ☐

2. Complete the following statements by ticking (✓) the last part of the sentence.

   a) Australia's wildlife has
      ☐ been the same for a very long time.
      ☐ changed a lot.
      ☐ become dangerous.

   b) 'Croc-wise' means knowing
      ☐ everything about Australia's crocodiles.
      ☐ what you must not do in crocodile areas.
      ☐ how to be on the day's menu.

   c) A crocodile
      ☐ can eat just once in a month.
      ☐ needs to eat regularly.
      ☐ needs to eat for many days.

   d) If you are on holiday in a crocodile area, you should
      ☐ look out for crocodiles before going swimming.
      ☐ picnic on the riverbank.
      ☐ stay away from the edge of the water as far as possible.

   e) If you are near a river and see a crocodile, you
      ☐ can shoot it because it is dangerous.
      ☐ must leave it alone because it is protected.
      ☐ must run away and get help.

f) In Australia some kangaroos
- [ ] attack in groups.
- [ ] live in trees.
- [ ] are bigger than a man.

g) An adult kangaroo can
- [ ] jump three metres long and hop at 60 mph.
- [ ] jump 9 meters high and hop at 60 kmh.
- [ ] hop at 60 kmh and jump 3 metres high.

h) Kangaroos were hunted
- [ ] because they caused damage.
- [ ] for food and for their skins.
- [ ] because there were too many of them.

i) In Australia there are
- [ ] almost two and half times as many kangaroos as people.
- [ ] twenty-eight million kangaroos.
- [ ] more people than kangaroos.

3. Match the parts of the sentence. Write the letter under the number in the answer box.

   (1) Saltwater crocodiles   a) live all over Australia.
   (2) Saltwater crocodiles can also   b) live dangerously.
   (3) If you swim in some rivers, you   c) live in groups.
   (4) Kangaroos   d) live in rivers, too.
   (5) Kangaroos usually   e) live in Australia.
   (6) Kangaroos have always been   f) live longer than some people.
       hunted by the people who

(1)	(2)	(3)	(4)	(5)	(6)

4. Imagine you have to make a list explaining how dangerous things are, or have been, in Australia. Read the text and then write in the grid which category you would put each thing under. D = dangerous, SD = seldom dangerous, ND = not dangerous.

   Australia has a large amount of colourful wildlife. Many species can only be found in this country, for example the kangaroos which are everywhere and damage things but don't hurt anyone. There were no cats, foxes or horses in Australia until the early settlers arrived. These harmless animals came with the Europeans but the early Europeans brought problems themselves. They introduced new illnesses, such as flu, into Australia which killed many Aborigines.

Australians have to be careful about a lot of things, however. Saltwater crocodiles eat many people every year, so do the sharks around the coast. Even sleeping has its dangers. Scorpions can climb up bed legs and give you a life-threatening sting and unless you are covered up in a net when you sleep you can be bitten by mosquitoes, which carry dangerous diseases. Many people worry about the snakes, too, but the few that can hurt people will only attack if they feel threatened.

Many other interesting animals and birds in Australia are never any problem to anyone, such as the cuddly-looking koalas and the emus which can't even fly.

kangaroos	
foxes	
the first white people	
saltwater crocodiles	
sharks	
scorpions	
snakes	
koalas	

Reading Test 4: An interview

TEEN	Interview	February 6

A *Could you introduce yourself, please?*
Yes, of course. My name in John Lumsden, I'm 26 and I come from Dublin in Ireland. I work just outside Munich as a biochemist at a biotechnology company.

B *Why did you come to Germany?*
Basically my girlfriend is German. We met in Ireland and lived there together for quite a long time but she didn't really like it, so we decided to move to Munich. Munich is where she's originally from. I wanted a change as well, a new job and a new career – something different.

C *What didn't your girlfriend like about Ireland?*
She didn't like Dublin because she thought it was too big and grey. She didn't like the weather in Ireland either, because it was always cloudy or raining. Ireland's always wet, you just can't escape the bad weather. If it's not actually raining, then it's going to rain soon.

D *Does everybody speak English in Ireland?*
Yes, they do but some people like to speak Gaelic. That's the original language in Ireland. But Irish people have strong accents and can be difficult to understand sometimes.

E *Do you have many different accents in Ireland?*
Yes, of course. In Dublin you don't hear a big difference in how people speak. There are people who speak very clearly and others who don't. But the people living in the country are often very difficult to understand because they speak very fast and not very clearly either. I think that's the same in many other countries, too.

F *Do you try to talk more clearly when you are in Germany?*
I think I do. I don't do it consciously but I do try and speak more slowly. I'm always worried that German people won't understand what I'm saying. I have to work with German people but I'm afraid my German isn't that good yet. I should try more but everyone here speaks such fantastic English.

G *Are the Irish bad at learning languages?*
I think they are. Very bad. At school you just don't see why you should learn a foreign language. Why learn French or German? Most people will never go to either country or need it at work and after a few years you have forgotten the small amount you have learnt anyway. I think German kids have it much harder. They have to learn English. It's all around them; on posters, in films, on TV and of course in songs and on the Internet. I'm a bit lazy, really. I still talk English with my girlfriend when we're at home in Germany. I think that the language which you first use when you meet someone is the one you always use. It just becomes a habit after a while. So even if I am totally fluent in German, I can still see us speaking English together.

H *What do you miss about Ireland?*
I miss the food. Well, not all of it, just some of the things we have in Ireland. I miss Guinness, of course, which you can get here in Munich but it's not the same as in Ireland. I also miss Irish bread and tea. When I visit home I always come back with lots of tea bags, Irish sausages and other things in my suitcase.

I *Do you do anything here in Germany that you wouldn't do in Ireland?*
Skiing. I've learnt to ski here and it's great fun. In Ireland you just don't have that opportunity. There's not often that much snow and when it does come it is very wet and of course we don't have any ski slopes. Around Munich it is just great. I think I'm much more active here than I was before when I was living in Dublin. I've even started going walking in the Alps. The most I did in Dublin was watch football on TV!

J *Have you got any hobbies or are there any special things you like to do?*

I like doing lots of things but have no real hobbies. I like to go to pop concerts if anyone good is playing. Last year I saw U2, which was fantastic – and Irish. I sometimes go and watch Bayern Munich play. Sometimes I just like to sit and read quietly. A lot depends upon my day at work. If it has been stressful then I usually do something very active, like running. But, if it was a normal day, then I just do normal sorts of things, like watching television, reading or going to a restaurant with my girlfriend. At the weekends I like to be outside, though, doing something in the fresh air.

Worksheet

1. If you wrote the interview as a text, which paragraphs (A–J) could you put under the headings in the grid? In some cases some headings have more than one paragraph. Two headings are not necessary.

   - Leisure time ☐
   - Language learning ☐
   - The working day ☐
   - Language and accents ☐
   - Reasons for moving ☐
   - The school system ☐
   - Talking to Germans ☐
   - The person's background ☐
   - The tastes of Ireland ☐

2. Tick (✓) the best answer to each question.

   a) What nationality is John?
      - ☐ German
      - ☐ Irish
      - ☐ English

   b) What was the main reason John left Dublin?
      - ☐ He wanted to work in Germany.
      - ☐ His girlfriend didn't like living in Ireland.
      - ☐ He and his girlfriend wanted to do something different.

   c) What is the weather like in John's country?
      - ☐ It snows a lot.
      - ☐ It's always grey.
      - ☐ It often rains or it looks like it is going to rain.

d) What do some people in Ireland speak?
   - [ ] English and German
   - [ ] French and German
   - [ ] Gaelic and English

e) Does John think people from Ireland are good at learning foreign languages?
   - [ ] No, he doesn't.
   - [ ] Yes, he does.
   - [ ] Some people are and some are not.

f) Why does John think German pupils have a hard time?
   - [ ] Because schools are harder.
   - [ ] Because they must learn English.
   - [ ] Because English is all around them.

g) Why don't John and his girlfriend speak German together?
   - [ ] Because they began speaking in English and just continued.
   - [ ] Because John's German is not very good.
   - [ ] Because John doesn't want to.

h) What does John miss about Ireland?
   - [ ] Everything.
   - [ ] Some things that you eat and drink.
   - [ ] The weather.

i) How has John's life changed?
   - [ ] He plays more football now.
   - [ ] He is not as active as when he was in Dublin.
   - [ ] He does more outside activities.

j) Does John have any hobbies?
   - [ ] No, he doesn't.
   - [ ] He and his girlfriend do a lot of sport.
   - [ ] Running.

3. Stelle John einem deutschen Freund vor. Dein deutscher Freund spricht kein Englisch, daher musst du ihm folgende Informationen über John auf Deutsch geben:
   - ▶ seinen Namen und seine Herkunft
   - ▶ was er macht
   - ▶ wo er jetzt wohnt
   - ▶ warum er nach Deutschland gekommen ist

Reading Test 5: Charities

In dieser Aufgabe erhältst du Informationen über vier Wohltätigkeitsorganisationen, die auf Spenden angewiesen sind. Zusätzlich erfährst du etwas über Menschen, die für Wohltätigkeitsorganisationen spenden. Beantworte alle Fragen so genau wie möglich.

Hinweise

Texte

ActionNow

ActionNow helps very poor families and their children in different parts of the world to have a better future. For many children in the Third World life is a daily fight to survive. With little food, polluted drinking water, disease and no schools the future is not good for these people. ActionNow helps these poor families and their children.
- It starts village schools so children can learn to read, write and do Maths.
- It helps with other projects, too, like providing the materials needed to bring fresh water to a village.

We help these poor families and their villages to help themselves so that they can have a better future.

The RNLI

The Royal National Lifeboat Institution is an emergency service for the sea.
We get no money from the government and we have few employees.
- *Most people are volunteers.*   • *Our members risk their lives every day saving other people.*

Sometimes a boat's engine has broken down or sometimes someone is very ill on a yacht and needs to go to hospital quickly, sometimes we rescue people who have fallen down a cliff, and sometimes we even have to rescue someone's pet that is stuck on the rocks.
▶ *The service is free but to keep it we need your money.*

WILD TRUST

Wild Trust was started about fifteen years ago. It helps to protect the countryside in many different ways.

- It looks after the birds and the animals found on its land.
- It tries to bring people closer to nature and shows them how important it is for everyone.
- We make special projects, too, for example building paths for countryside walks.
- We even have our own hospital for injured animals and birds that are found not just by us but by people in the area.

Our future plans are to buy a forest and keep it as a place of special interest for people to enjoy. We also want to try and protect an area of the coast so that people can see how it should be and not full of litter and tourists.

Don't Fall Down

Have you ever seen wonderful old buildings not looked after? They look dirty, high grass takes over the gardens and ivy grows quickly up the walls and over the roofs. The roofs then often collapse, windows become broken and walls get damaged. Suddenly, a beautiful old building becomes a ruin.

▶ We want to look after these historic buildings.
We like to rebuild them and make them beautiful again.

Sometimes they become museums or activity centres but whatever they become they are given a life once again. Instead of being a horrible broken-down eyesore, they are returned to how they once were. If you support Don't Fall Down, then you're supporting your heritage for future generations to enjoy.

Kompetenzbereich: Reading

Worksheet

1. Which charity do you think the following people give money to?

   a) Mr Davies is an architect. He works in London but loves going into the countryside looking at castles and other interesting buildings. He always takes photographs of them and sometimes he imagines how he could make them into something else.

   b) Jenny and her husband met when they were in Kenya. He was working as a doctor in a small village hospital and she was teaching the children there. She laughs now about the school because it just had one classroom and fifty children of all different ages. She now works in a school with over 1,000 pupils.

   c) The Smith family have got two children. Their house is always untidy because they also have two dogs and two cats that never stop fighting each other. They have a big garden and live in a small village. Mr Smith made a pond in his garden and the children are always playing outside somewhere. The whole family loves riding horses.

   d) Mike loves the weekends. Last year he went on a sailing course on a lake near where he lives. Now he and a friend go sailing every weekend. The lake was boring once he had learnt to sail so now they go to Brancaster which is on the coast. The coast there is beautiful and he loves the peace and quiet. It is fun sailing on the sea but it can be dangerous.

   ActionNow _____
   The RNLI _____
   Wild Trust _____
   Don't Fall Down _____

2. Look at the photographs. Which photograph goes with which charity organisation? Write the number of the photograph under the name of the charity. Some photographs are not needed.

ActionNow	The RNLI	Wild Trust	Don't Fall Down

3. Write one or two sentences in English to explain what each charity does.

ActionNow

_____
_____

The RNLI

_____
_____

Wild Trust

_____
_____

Don't Fall Down

_____
_____

4. Answer the following questions about the charities in German in full sentences.

   a) Was können die armen Kinder hauptsächlich in der Schule lernen?

   b) Warum braucht die RNLI unser Geld?

   c) Welche zwei Dinge will Wild Trust in Zukunft tun?

   d) An welcher Art von Gebäuden ist Don't Fall Down interessiert?

Reading Test 6: The Royal Theatre

Bei dieser Übung werden dir drei Annoncen über verschiedene Aufführungen an einem englischen Theater vorgelegt. Beachte beim Lesen besonders die verwendeten Abkürzungen. In der ersten Aufgabe musst du sagen, welche Aufführung die Personen jeweils besuchen würden. Achte bei deinen Antworten besonders auf die Bedürfnisse der einzelnen Personen.

Hinweise

Texte

Wed 27th July – Sat 5th August

Robinson Crusoe

Wonderful family entertainment to begin the summer holidays. Everyone knows the story of Robinson Crusoe and how he gets shipwrecked in a storm and then how he has to live alone on a small island. But this story starts before Daniel Defoe's famous book. First the hero is attacked by pirates, then he goes to America. After that, when sailing to South America, he finally ends up on the island by himself until he saves Man Friday from the cannibals, who arrive for their barbecue! There's lots of fun for all the family. It's a story for anyone over 7 years old.

Times: Mon – Fri: 7.00 p.m.; Sat + Sun: 2.30 p.m., 7.15 p.m.
Duration: 150 minutes

Prices: Adults: £ 6.50
Young people 11–18, students and grandparents: £ 4.50
Children under 11: £ 2.50

(to be) shipwrecked = schiffbrüchig sein; duration = Laufzeit / Dauer

Mon 7th August – Sun 20th August

Summer Holiday

A real summer holiday musical for the family. It makes you laugh, it makes you happy and it makes you sing the songs for weeks after you've left the theatre. It's just fun, fun and more fun, with lots of 50s and 60s music, too.
A group of young people decide to go 'where the sun shines brightly' in a red, London double-decker bus which they have converted into a very big camper. They travel across Europe having fun and enjoying themselves but they're always being chased by the mother of Bobby, one of the young people. Bobby isn't just any normal girl, she's a famous singer in disguise. Her agent also wants her back in England so he, too, wants to catch up with the group of young people.

Times:
Mon – Thurs: 7.30 p.m. (Fri: no performance)
Sat + Sun: 2.15 p.m., 7.30 p.m. – Duration: 135 minutes

Prices:
Adults: £ 10.50, Young people 11–18, students: £ 8.50, Children: £ 4.50

Mon 21st August – Mon 28th August

Macbeth

Witches, blood, murder. What more does anyone want for a good night in the theatre? Shakespeare's Macbeth has something for everyone. The play starts with Macbeth on his way home after a battle meeting three horrible, old, dirty witches in the middle of a storm.
They tell him he will become King of Scotland, which Macbeth wants very much. Macbeth and his wife murder the King and then Macbeth takes over. But the ending is not a happy one for Lady Macbeth or the new King of Scotland. Fast, brutal and the best theatre play this year.

Times: Every evening: 8.15 p.m. – Duration: 150 minutes
Prices: Adults: £ 12.50, Young people 16–18, students: £ 9.50
         Not suitable for children under 16

Worksheet

1. Which theatre performance would each of these people or families go to: A – Robinson Crusoe, B – Summer Holiday or C – Macbeth?   A B C

   a) Mr and Mrs Jones like Shakespeare very much.
   b) Mrs Smith and her two children want to go to something that is cheap.
   c) Mr and Mrs Williams have a 16-year-old daughter. They all like musicals.
   d) David and his friend are going to Europe in the summer. They thought this would be fun for them to see.
   e) The Jackson family have a son who is 16 and a daughter who is 13. They all like going to the theatre together but do not like musicals.
   f) Jane's grandma wants to take her to the theatre, but she does not want to spend a lot of money.
   g) Susan and Karen do not want to go to something where there are children.
   h) Luke wants to take his brother to the theatre. But they can only go on a Friday and the performance must finish before 10 o'clock.
   i) Henry and his wife grew up in the 1950s and the early 1960s. They like seeing happy things.
   j) Harry and Sally are students and are studying English.

2. Answer the following questions about the theatre performances.

   a) Who wrote Robinson Crusoe?
      - [ ] Man Friday
      - [ ] Shakespeare
      - [ ] Daniel Defoe

   b) When do the afternoon performances of Robinson Crusoe finish?
      - [ ] 2.30 p.m.
      - [ ] 5.00 p.m.
      - [ ] 5.30 p.m.

   c) How much does it cost for two adults and two children, 7 and 13, to go to Robinson Crusoe?
      - [ ] £ 17.50
      - [ ] £ 20.00
      - [ ] £ 18.00

   d) What day can't you go to see Summer Holiday?
      - [ ] Monday
      - [ ] Friday
      - [ ] Saturday

   e) Who is Bobby?
      - [ ] She's a typical young woman.
      - [ ] She's an agent.
      - [ ] She's someone famous.

   f) Who do the witches talk to?
      - [ ] the King of Scotland
      - [ ] themselves
      - [ ] Macbeth

3. Tell your friend in German what the three theatre performances are about. Give short summaries. You do not have to translate everything.

   Robinson Crusoe

   _____
   _____
   _____

   Summer Holiday

   _____
   _____
   _____

Macbeth
___
___

4. Answer the following questions in English using the information from the adverts. You must write in full sentences.

   a) What do the cannibals want to do on the beach?
   ___
   ___

   b) Are there any age restrictions for seeing *Robinson Crusoe*?
   ___
   ___

   c) What kind of music is played in *Summer Holiday*?
   ___
   ___

   d) Why do people not know who Bobby really is?
   ___
   ___

   e) What has happened before Macbeth meets the witches?
   ___
   ___

   f) What happens to the King of Scotland and who becomes the next one?
   ___
   ___

Reading Test 7: Scene2

Hier siehst du eine Annonce für eine neue Zeitschrift für junge Leute. Die meisten unbekannten Wörter müsstest du aus dem Textzusammenhang erschließen können.

Hinweise

Scene2

Scene2 is a monthly magazine for young people. It has everything young people want – boys or girls. Young people for us are not kids, they're people with very special interests. We don't have problem pages and we don't have silly love stories. Instead, we have what's going on now – the scene!

Music
We look at what's new, we have interviews with the famous and the not so famous. We show you what you need to know about being in this business. How do you get into it? Who do you contact? And what you should and shouldn't do. We write about new songs and CDs and give the backgrounds to them.

Fashion
What's cool? Fashion is great on thin models but what about normal people who haven't got the money for designer wear. We'll take you shopping. We'll show you what you can buy and where it's cheap. We get to the trends before other people. So, if you want to be cool – read Scene2.

News
Boring? No, not really. There's nothing more boring than not being able to talk about anything especially what's going on in the big world. Mobiles, sport and television all have their place but so does the environment, politics and industry. We'll bring you the facts; short, easy to understand and full of information. You'll have more than enough to talk about in the future.

Leaving school
What next? Work or more education? Or travel abroad for a year? What can you do with your life? What are the opportunities for young people? We'll show you how to get your first job or an apprenticeship[1]. We'll give you good tips and also explain to you what not to do. We'll have interviews with young people who started with nothing and are now successful. We'll give you lots of ideas of what you can really do – have you ever thought of working for six months with children in a third-world country or helping wild animals survive? Scene2 has it all, and more.

More
Yes, more. We have everything that young people want. How to buy your first car. What to look for and which cars are the best. How to pass your driving test. Where are great holiday places for fun – discos and nightlife – or for active holidays – snowboarding, climbing or mountain biking? We have everything and much, much more.

Text

✂---

Scene2

To order your copy of Scene2 complete the following form and send it to:
The Editor, Scene2, 3 Wolverton Road, Bath, BA56 7TZ.

Subscription details
Full name (Mr/Mrs/Miss/Ms) ....

Address ....

Date of birth	....	Town	....
Telephone	....	Postcode	....
e-mail	....	Country	....

No. of issues required: 6 months ☐ £ 25 or € 37   12 months ☐ £ 45 or € 70

We'll send a free copy to a friend, too. Just provide all the details as above.

✂---

1 apprenticeship = Lehre

Worksheet

1. Right or wrong or not in the text? Tick (✓) the correct box.

                                                                                                     right wrong not in the text

   a) There are twelve magazines every year.
   b) Scene2 is a girl's magazine.
   c) The magazine is about things happening today.
   d) There are a lot of music jobs offered in the magazine.
   e) The diets are very good.
   f) There is a section about clothes.
   g) Scene2 thinks the news is not necessary for young people.
   h) The magazine tells you about the things you can do after leaving school.
   i) The magazine has many different topics for young people.
   j) If you want Scene2 you have to telephone the magazine.
   k) It is more expensive to get a year's subscription than a half year's.
   l) The free gift is very useful.
   m) You can get one magazine for a friend when you order the magazine.

2. Answer the next questions in full sentences.

   a) What happens to new songs and CDs in the magazine?
   _____
   _____

   b) Why does Scene2 put the news in its magazine?
   _____
   _____

   c) The magazine has interviews with famous and not so famous people in music. It also interviews other people. Who?
   _____
   _____

   d) What could you do for half a year after school?
   _____
   _____

   e) What types of holiday can you find out about?
   _____
   _____

3. Complete the subscription form. Also address the envelope in an English style.
   To order your copy of Scene2 complete the following form and send it to: The Editor, Scene2, 3 Wolverton Road, Bath, BA56 7TZ.

   Subscription details
   Full name (Mr/Mrs/Miss/Ms)

   Address
   Town
   Postcode
   Date of birth
   Telephone
   e-mail
   No. of issues required: 6 months ☐ £25 or € 37   12 months ☐ £45 or € 70

   _____
   _____
   _____
   _____

4. What do the following words mean? Write in full sentences.
   a) an interview (line 10)

   b) a third-world country (lines 43/44)

   c) nightlife (line 51)

5. You want to tell your friend about the magazine and the free copy. What would you say in German?

   a) Tell your friend what the magazine is called and how often it is published.

   b) Give your friend some examples of the content of the magazine.

   c) Explain how long you are going to subscribe to the magazine and how much it costs.

6. Your English friend says some things about the magazine. How would you reply in English?

   a) I think the music will be terrible – boring pop music, nothing for me.

   b) I don't have a lot of money, therefore the fashion part won't interest me.

   c) I never understand the news.

   d) I would like to do something different before I start to work but I don't know what.

   e) Sometimes I want to go on holiday with my friends but we never know where we can go.

Reading Test 8: The Australian Aborigines

Hier sollst du einen Sachtext lesen, verstehen und bearbeiten. Unterstreiche beim zweiten Lesen alle Schlüsselbegriffe, denn diese werden dir sicherlich beim Bearbeiten der Aufgaben hilfreich sein.

A The word 'aborigine' means 'the people who were here from the beginning', which, of course, in Australia they were. In fact, Aborigines have been living in Australia for at least 40,000 years. Until Europeans arrived in Australia the Aborigines had lived there very happily. They usually lived in family groups known as tribes. These could be very small with 6 to 10 people or very large camps with up to 400 people.

B Land is very important for the Aborigines. They believe that it is made for them by their ancestors and, therefore, much of it is sacred, for example Uluru which white people often call Ayers Rock. In the past, Aborigines lived from the land of their ancestors. They were hunters, fishermen and gatherers. A gatherer was a collector – a person who collected food such as eggs, berries and insects. Aborigines were not farmers, they did not have fields or animals, so every day the men went hunting or fishing and the women and children did the gathering. This meant their food was always fresh but they had to understand nature very well. They had to know when and where they could get something to eat, for example. The food that was caught or found was shared among the tribe.

C All adult Aboriginal men were equal but within the 'families' there were leaders called 'Elders'. The Elders gave advice and were listened to. They knew the old ways, the traditions and the laws of the Aborigines, and were respected. Not all old people were Elders, however. Elders were usually only the people who were clever, for example 'doctors', or who had a special skill.

D Unfortunately, since 1788, the history of the Aborigines has not been a very happy one. In 1788, the Europeans arrived in Australia and made the Aborigines leave their lands. The Europeans wanted the land for themselves to start new lives, usually as farmers. If the Aborigines did not leave, they were shot and killed – and that happened to a lot of them. Also, the Europeans brought illnesses that had not existed in Australia before, for example influenza *(Grippe),* which killed many more.

E The Aborigines had a poor life now. They were made to live in special areas and half-cast *(Mischling)* children were taken away from the Aboriginal parent, usually this was the mother. These children were then given to white people and were made to grow up in the 'white' way. This happened until almost the end of the last century. Today, these Aborigines do not know who their 'family' is – many do not even know who their parents or grandparents are.

F Most Aborigines are discriminated against and often cannot find jobs. Many start drinking alcohol and have poor lives. Most have lost their culture forever. The Australian government is slowly trying to make things better for the Aborigines but there is still a lot of work to do to help them to get better, fairer and equal lives.

Worksheet

1. The text has got 6 paragraphs. In the grid below there are 8 headings. Decide which is the best heading for each paragraph (A–F) and write the letter in the answer space. Two headings are wrong.

   The first settlers ☐
   Made to be white ☐
   Having families ☐
   From hunters to farmers ☐
   The original people ☐
   Living off the land ☐
   The situation today ☐
   Family leaders ☐

2. Which answer is right? Tick (✓) the correct box.

   a) How long have Aborigines been living in Australia?
      ☐ a short time
      ☐ a very long time
      ☐ since arriving from Europe

   b) Where did Aborigines live?
      ☐ in large villages
      ☐ with many different families
      ☐ in family groups

   c) What is one of the most important things for Aborigines?
      ☐ Uluru
      ☐ their land
      ☐ being able to hunt

   d) Who would be gatherers?
      ☐ anyone who wanted to pick berries
      ☐ old people who could not fish or hunt
      ☐ women and children

   e) Why was it important that the Aborigines understood nature very well?
      ☐ so they knew where food was at any time of the year
      ☐ so they did not get cold
      ☐ so they could share their food with everybody

f) What describes Elders the best?
- [ ] the old people in an Aboriginal tribe
- [ ] the people who could remember the old ways
- [ ] older Aborigines with particular skills which made them be respected

g) Why did many Aborigines die when the Europeans arrived?
- [ ] the Europeans did not allow them any food
- [ ] the Europeans killed many and brought with them diseases
- [ ] because they had to leave their homes and go away

h) What happened to many children with white fathers and Aboriginal mothers?
- [ ] they grew up with their fathers
- [ ] they were taken away from their mothers and brought up in white families
- [ ] they were given to their grandparents to look after

i) Why is the Australian government trying to help the Aborigines?
- [ ] because they were badly discriminated against and now have many other problems, too
- [ ] because they have lost their way
- [ ] because many of them drink alcohol

3. Combine the matching parts of the sentences. Write the correct letters under the numbers in the answer box.

   (1) The Aborigines were very happy
   (2) Uluru is the name
   (3) In their 'families'
   (4) Farming was work
   (5) A lot of Aborigines died
   (6) Many Aborigines are unhappy

   a) because they have lost their old ways.
   b) for the Europeans.
   c) for Ayers Rock.
   d) until the Europeans arrived.
   e) all men were equal.
   f) because the Europeans brought new diseases to Australia.

(1)	(2)	(3)	(4)	(5)	(6)

4. Answer the following questions in full sentences.
   a) Why is land important to an Aborigine?

   b) What type of people were the Aborigines?

   c) Why did the Aborigines search for food every day?

   d) Why did the Aborigines' happy way of living end suddenly?

   e) Why do some Aborigines not know their own parents or other family members?

3 Kompetenzbereich: Sprechen (English in use)

Die Aufgabenstellungen, die dir im Unterricht und in Prüfungen zum Kompetenzbereich „Sprechen" (English in use) begegnen, sind sehr vielfältig. Ziel dieser Aufgaben ist es, deinen persönlichen Wortschatz zu testen, deine Kenntnisse grammatikalischer Strukturen zu überprüfen und du musst hier deine Sprechfähigkeiten in der Fremdsprache Englisch unter Beweis stellen.

3.1 Strategien zum Kompetenzbereich „Sprechen" (English in use)

Grammatik ist kein direkter Bestandteil deiner Abschlussprüfung, wird aber indirekt in verschiedenen Aufgaben geprüft und ist generell eine wichtige Grundlage für das Beherrschen einer Fremdsprache. Um deine Grammatikkenntnisse aufzufrischen findest du auf den Seiten 85–106 dieses Buches eine Kurzgrammatik.

Eine weitere Fähigkeit, die im Bereich „Sprechen" (English in use) geprüft wird, kennst du schon aus den vorherigen Kapiteln: Dort musstest du bereits einige Male englische Fragen auf deutsch beantworten und damit zeigen, dass du den Sachverhalt im englischen Text verstanden hast. Der englische Text musste dann von dir auf deutsch wiedergegeben werden. So konntest du keine Fehler in der Fremdsprache Englisch machen und hattest eine sehr gute Möglichkeit, Punkte zu sammeln. In diesem Kapitel musst du nun eine alltägliche Situation, die dir auf deutsch präsentiert wird, in englischer Sprache wiedergeben. So wird überprüft, wie gut du Englisch wirklich *sprechen* kannst.

Es ist wichtig, dass du dich hier von den deutschen Vorgaben löst und dir überlegst, was die Aussage im deutschen ist. — Arbeitsschritt 1

Im nächsten Schritt überlegst du dir, was die passende englische Wendung ist, um diese Aussage auch in englischer Sprache wiederzugeben. Auf keinen Fall darfst du versuchen, den Text Wort für Wort zu übersetzen. — Arbeitsschritt 2

Der nächste Schritt ist dann, eine richtige Konversation auf Englisch zu führen. — Arbeitsschritt 3

TIPP
- Löse dich vom deutschen Text.
- Überlege, was die Aussage des Textes ist.
- Suche die passenden englischen Wendungen.
- Übersetze den Text nicht einfach Wort für Wort ins Englische.

Kompetenzbereich: Sprechen (English in use)

Ein wichtiger Bestandteil dieses gesamten Kompetenzbereiches ist das Beherrschen von Vokabeln. Eine gründliche Vokabelkenntnis ist für alle Aufgaben erforderlich, die dir in diesem Bereich begegnen, nicht nur für Aufgaben, in denen direkt dein Wortschatz abgefragt wird, sondern auch für den Prüfungsteil in dem du deine Sprechfähigkeiten zeigen sollst oder in einem anderen Teil der Realschulabschlussprüfung, wenn du eigene kleine Texte verfassen musst. Es ist wichtig, dass du in diesem Bereich langfristig und nachhaltig übst. Vokabeln zu lernen ist nicht gerade spannend, aber unerlässlich für den Erwerb einer Fremdsprache. Je größer dein aktiver Wortschatz ist, je mehr Wörter du also in der Fremdsprache kennst und selbst in Gesprächen oder beim Schreiben anwenden kannst, desto treffender und abwechslungsreicher kannst du dich in der Fremdsprache ausdrücken. Um den aktiven Wortschatz zu vergrößern, gibt es verschiedene Methoden, die dir im Folgenden vorgestellt werden.

Methode 1

Natürlich ist zunächst einmal das **Vokabelheft** zu erwähnen. Du weißt, wie es funktioniert: Richte dir auf jeder Doppelseite drei Spalten ein, eine für den englischen Begriff, eine für die deutsche Bedeutung und eine, in der du den Ausdruck in einem Beispielsatz verwendest. Zum Lernen deckst du dann jeweils eine Spalte ab.

Methode 2

Wesentlich effektiver ist es, die **Vokabeln auf Karteikarten** zu notieren. Schreibe den englischen Begriff auf die Vorderseite der Karte. Notiere dazu auch einen englischen Satz, in dem die Vokabel vorkommt. So lernst du gleich die Verwendung der Vokabel mit. Notiere auch sonst alles, was zu der Vokabel gehört (z. B. bei Verben nicht nur den Infinitiv, sondern auch die verschiedenen Personalformen „I …, you …, he/she/it …" oder die Präpositionen, die bestimmte Verben nach sich ziehen). Auf der Rückseite der Karteikarte schreibst du die deutsche Bedeutung der Vokabel auf.
Die Karteikartenmethode hat im Vergleich zum herkömmlichen Vokabelheft Vorteile:

▶ Du kannst die Karteikarten drei Stapeln zuordnen.
Stapel 1: **Wörter, die neu für dich sind.** Diese Wörter solltest du mindestens jeden zweiten Tag durchgehen. Lies dabei auch immer den englischen Satz durch, den du auf der Karteikarte notiert hast. Manchmal ist es leichter, sich ein Wort im Satzzusammenhang zu merken, als als einzelne Vokabel. Sobald du die neue Vokabel kennst, legst du sie auf Stapel 2 ab.
Stapel 2: **Wörter, die du noch nicht so sicher im Kopf hast.** Diesen Stapel solltest du regelmäßig durchgehen und dabei die Vokabeln üben. Wenn du eine Vokabel sicher weißt, legst du sie auf Stapel 3 ab.
Stapel 3: **Wörter, die du schon sehr gut beherrschst.** Diesen Stapel solltest du hin und wieder einmal durchblättern, um zu sehen, ob du alle Vokabeln noch richtig beherrschst.

▶ Du kannst die Karteikarten je nach augenblicklicher Lernsituation nach **Wortfeldern** (z. B. weather: wind, snow, sun) oder nach **Wortfamilien** (z. B. business, businessman, businesswoman, busy) ordnen. Dabei bist du sehr flexibel und kannst die Wortfelder bzw. Wortfamilien jederzeit erweitern bzw. umbauen.

Du kannst natürlich auch kreativ sein und dir deine eigene Methode zum Vokabellernen ausdenken. Das macht natürlich am meisten Spaß und bringt langfristig gesehen sicherlich den besten Lernerfolg.

▶ Zeichne dir Mindmaps zu gelernten Vokabeln. Du kannst sie – auch hier wieder abhängig von deiner augenblicklichen Lernsituation – nach Wortfeldern oder Wortfamilien zusammenstellen. Diese Mindmaps kannst du an zentralen Stellen in deinem Zimmer aufhängen. Jedes Mal, wenn du daran vorbeikommst, gehst du die entsprechenden Vokabeln im Kopf durch.

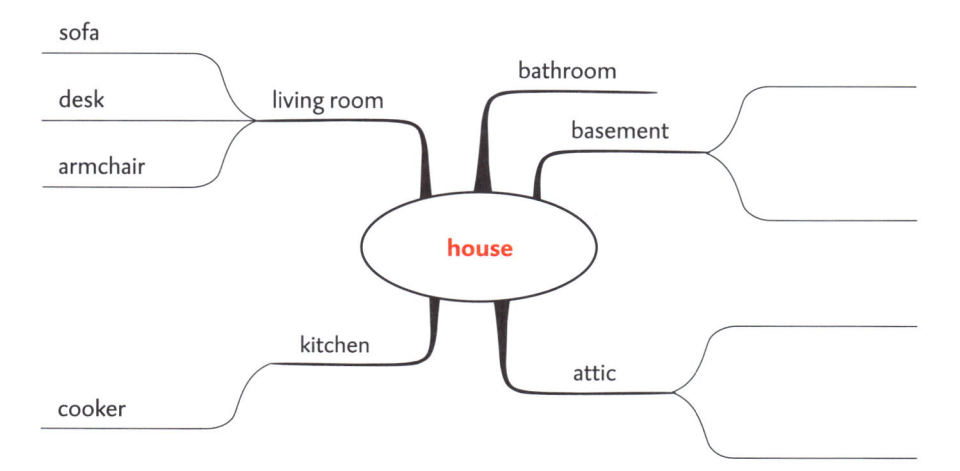

Methode 3

Beispiel

```
sofa
desk      living room          bathroom
armchair                       basement
                  house
          kitchen              attic
cooker
```

▶ Jedes Mal, wenn du eine neue Vokabel gelernt hast, schreibst du den Begriff auf einen Zettel und befestigst ihn am entsprechenden Gegenstand bei dir zu Hause. So klebst du beispielsweise einen Zettel mit dem Begriff „cupboard" an euren Küchenschrank. Das funktioniert zum Teil auch mit abstrakten Begriffen: Die Vokabel „proud" könntest du z. B. an das Regalfach heften, in dem deine Schulsachen sind. Denn sicherlich bist du doch „stolz" darauf, dass du in der Schule schon so weit gekommen bist, oder? Mit dieser Zettelmethode kannst du neue Vokabeln jedenfalls ganz einfach nebenbei, quasi „im Vorbeigehen" trainieren.

▶ Versuche immer wieder, die neuen Vokabeln anzuwenden, am besten in einem vollständigen englischen Satz. Wenn du dich mit Klassenkameraden unterhältst, könnt ihr daraus vielleicht ein richtiges Spiel machen.

Welche Methode du auch anwendest oder mit anderen Strategien kombinierst, lerne nie zu viele Vokabeln auf einmal! Am besten ist es, wenn du neue Vokabeln immer in kleinen Gruppen von sechs bis sieben Wörtern lernst. Lies sie dir zunächst ein paar Mal durch, wiederhole sie auch laut – in einer modernen Fremdsprache kommt es auch auf die korrekte Aussprache an! – und lege sie dann für etwa 20 Minuten zur Seite. Dann fängst du von vorne an. Diese Pausen sind wichtig, damit sich das gerade Gelernte „setzen" kann. So wird es dir ein Leichtes sein, bald einen großen englischen Wortschatz anzusammeln.

TIPP

- Lerne langfristig. In der Fremdsprache einen großen aktiven Wortschatz zu haben, ist sehr wichtig.
- Lege ein Vokabelheft an oder notiere deine Vokabeln auf Karteikarten. Lerne die Vokabeln im Satzzusammenhang.
- Sei kreativ beim Vokabellernen: Zeichne Mindmaps, beschrifte die Gegenstände in deinem Zimmer.
- Lerne deine Vokabeln immer in Sechser- oder Siebenergruppen. Mache zwischen deinen Lerneinheiten regelmäßig kleine Pausen, damit sich das Gelernte „setzen" kann. Trainiere beim Lernen auch die Aussprache.

3.2 Häufige Aufgabenstellungen zum Kompetenzbereich „Sprechen" (English in use)

Opposites and synonyms

Mit einer Aufgabenformulierung wie *Find opposites* wirst du aufgefordert, das Gegenteil zu einem vorgegebenen Wort zu finden. Manchmal musst du auch *synonyms* zu verschiedenen Begriffen angeben. *Synonyms* sind Wörter, die in etwa das Gleiche bedeuten wie das Ausgangswort.

Es werden dir entweder einzelne Worte vorgegeben, zu denen du das Gegenteil *(opposite)* oder ein Synonym *(synonym)* finden musst oder dir werden kleine Texte vorgegeben, in denen Wörter markiert sind, zu denen *synonyms* gefunden werden müssen.

Beispiel

Find synonyms for the words underlined.

I went to my brother's wedding with a <u>small</u> whole in my shoe. I didn't notice it <u>at first</u> but it had been raining and when we were <u>standing</u> outside the church, I felt my foot slowly getting wetter and wetter and then freezing cold. It was really <u>horrible</u> but I couldn't do anything about it.

small	*tiny / little*
at first	*initially / straight away*
standing	*waiting*
horrible	*terrible / awful*

Missing words and word grids

Anhand von Lückentexten oder einzelnen Lückensätzen wird geprüft, wie groß dein Wortschatz ist. Dabei kann die Aufgabe Hilfestellungen enthalten oder auch nicht. In der Regel befindet sich unter dem Lückentext ein Raster *(word grid)* mit verschiedenen Lösungsmöglichkeiten für jede Lücke. Du musst dort das korrekte Wort herausfinden. Bei dieser Aufgabe werden deine Grammatik- und deine Wortschatzkenntnisse überprüft.

Fill in the missing word from each sentence.
It is very wet and ___windy___ . (1)
Many Australians live near the ___coast___ . (2)
From the top of the mountain there was a good ___view___ . (3)

Beispiel

1	windy	rainy	wavy
2	beech	coast	waves
3	sight	view	look

Sprechen

Hier musst du unter Beweis stellen, dass du auch über Sprechfertigkeiten im Englischen verfügst. Dir werden meist alltägliche Situationen auf Deutsch präsentiert und du musst zeigen, dass du in dieser Situation angemessen auf Englisch reagieren kannst.

Dictionary work

Eine wichtige Grundkompetenz besteht darin, mit einem Wörterbuch umgehen zu können. Deshalb wird im Englischunterricht ausführlich geübt, wie man in einem Wörterbuch nachschlägt und wie man den für die Situation passenden Ausdruck findet. Auch in deiner Abschlussprüfung musst du diese Fertigkeit unter Beweis stellen. Dazu musst du zunächst einmal wissen, was die in den Wörterbüchern verwendeten Abkürzungen bedeuten. In der Einleitung zu jedem Wörterbuch findest du eine Liste mit den benutzten Abkürzungen und ihren Erklärungen. Mit dieser Liste solltest du dich vertraut machen.

3.3 Hilfreiche Wendungen zum Kompetenzbereich „Sprechen" (English in use)

Fragen stellen

was/was für ein(e)/welche(r, s)?	what?
wer/wen/wem?	who?
wo/wohin/woher?	where?
warum?	why?
wie?	how?
Gibt es …? Hast du/Haben sie …?	Are there any …?
Wie lange dauert es …?	How long does it take …?
Kann ich bitte … haben?	Can I have … please?
Können sie/Kannst du mir … zeigen?	Can you show me …?
Wie wäre es …? (Vorschlag)	What about …?
Wie komme ich zu/zur …?	How can I get to …?
Wie teuer ist es …?	How much is it …?

Meinung vertreten

Ich denke, dass …	I think/believe/expect/imagine …
Ich denke nicht, dass …	I don't think …
Meiner Meinung nach …	In my opinion …
Ich stimme dir zu.	I agree with you.
Ich stimme dir nicht zu.	I don't agree with you.
Ich würde gerne …	I'd like to …
Ich würde lieber …	I'd prefer to …
Ich habe nichts dagegen.	I don't mind.
Das ist schade.	That's a pity.

3.4 Übungsaufgaben zum Kompetenzbereich „Sprechen" (English in use)

1. Look at the photograph of an English house. Write in the missing words. Try to remember the prepositions of place, for example 'in front of'. You have the first letter of the prepositions to help you.

   For example: A _____ the _____ there is a small _____.

   <u>Above</u> the <u>door</u> there is a small <u>roof</u>.

   The car is standing on the _____.

   The car is in front of the _____.

   The house is b_____ the garage.

   The front door is b_____ the garage and the window.

   The front door is n_____ ____ the garage.

   I__ _____ ___ the house there is a large tree in a small _____.

2. Some words rhyme and have **almost the same** spelling, for example: *house – mouse*. Some words rhyme and have **different** spelling, for example: *what – yacht (Segelschiff/Yacht)*.
In the box there are **six** words that sound the same as **six** other words. Can you find them? There are many words you do not need.

   wear, whale, bike, water, seat, care, town, tear, great, string, round, sail, ring, trouble, feel, bubble, meal, table, meet, station

   _____ – _____
   _____ – _____
   _____ – _____
   _____ – _____
   _____ – _____
   _____ – _____

3. Read the sentences carefully. Fill in the words that are missing. You are shown how many letters are needed.
   For example: It is very wet and w_i_ _n_ _d_ _y_ today.

   a) Every m_ _ _ _ _ _ the man gets into his c_ _ and d_ _ _ _ _ _ to work.

   b) At work he always s_ _ _ at the same d_ _ _ _.

   c) Sarah likes working with c_ _ _ _ _ _ _, she's a teacher.

   d) The s_ _ _ was very deep and we could go skiing.

   e) The h_ _ _ _ where she lived was very b_ _.

   f) My bus was l_ _ _ this m_ _ _ _ _ _.

   g) I r_ _ _ my bike to school yesterday.

   h) I like t_ _ _ _ _ _ _ _ by car but I don't like f_ _ _ _ _.

4. Join the people to their countries, the language they speak and a city in that country
   For example: Australians – Australia – English – Sydney

   (the) French, England, (the) Spanish, German, (the) Italians, Germany, Berlin, New York, (the) Americans, Dutch, Rome, (the) Germans, Turkey, French, Amsterdam, (the) Dutch, ~~(the) English~~, Italy, (the) Turkish, English, English, the Netherlands, Istanbul, America, Spanish, Italian, France, Paris, Spain, Madrid, London, Turkish

the people	the country	the language	a city
(the) English			

Fill in the missing words from the following sentences.

a) Jenny comes from London. She's _____ and she speaks _____.

b) Jan comes from Amsterdam in _____. He's _____.

c) Ismael is _____. He lives in Istanbul. Istanbul is in _____.

d) Pierre loves spaghetti. He comes from _____. He only speaks _____.

e) Louisa lives in Paris. She's _____. Most people in _____ only speak _____.

f) Madrid is in _____. The people who live in Madrid are _____.

5. Each job has got something to do with an object, people or animals. Join them together.

   (1) doctor   (A) restaurant
   (2) vet   (B) boat
   (3) pilot   (C) children
   (4) builder   (D) radio
   (5) mechanic   (E) plane
   (6) teacher   (F) house
   (7) sailor   (G) cars
   (8) DJ   (H) hospital
   (9) chef   (I) animals

1	2	3	4	5	6	7	8	9

Kompetenzbereich: Sprechen (English in use) | 57

6. Complete the text by selecting the correct word from the grid. For each space (1-20) you are given three possibilities to choose from.

_____ (1) is the capital of England. It's a very _____ (2) city with _____ (3) interesting _____ (4). It's also a _____ (5) with a great nightlife. There are lots of _____ (6), theatres, and, of course, clubs, _____ (7) and pubs. There is _____ (8) lots to do and see. You can _____ (9) Buckingham Palace or see Downing Street where the prime minister _____ (10). There is also a big wheel called the London Eye. From the _____ (11) of it there is a _____ (12) view over London. But it is very _____ (13)! The _____ (14) way to see London, though, is by _____ (15) or by a city tour on a _____ (16) double-decker _____ (17). London is a _____ (18) city, everyone should _____ (19) it _____ (20).

1	London	Londone	Londen
2	larger	large	largest
3	much	many	more
4	building's	building	buildings
5	city	town	area
6	cinemas	cinema	cinema's
7	restaurants	resterants	restaurents
8	forever	always	seldom
9	visits	visit	visited
10	had lived	is living	lives
11	top	head	bottom
12	fanatic	fantastic	fantasy
13	high	height	higher
14	better	good	best
15	foot	food	feet
16	red	blue	green
17	buses	coach	bus
18	wonderful	wunderful	wonderfully
19	visiting	visited	visit
20	anytime	sometime	sometimes

7. Complete the following text. Think carefully about what type of word is needed, for example a verb form, an adverb, a noun or an adjective. The grid offers you several possible solutions for each gap. Choose which solution is correct and fill in the missing words.

I really like music. I have never played a _____ (1) instrument in my life but I have always _____ (2) songs interesting. For me they _____ (3) in two ways. First, I find that as time _____ (4) songs remind me of things that happened in my life. I remember my first girlfriend, for example, by a _____ (5) that was always on the radio at that time. Secondly, I'm _____ (6) with how people _____ (7) to write the songs they did and what the texts really mean. It was only _____ (8), for example, that I discovered what Bob Marley _____ (9) about with his song 'Buffalo Soldier'. Buffalo soldiers were Africans who _____ (10) for the Americans against the Indians. Eminem is also a _____ (11) _____ (12) singer-songwriter. Although I _____ (13) won't remember any of his songs in the future, many young people can relate to the _____ (14) of feelings in his lyrics and enjoy his live _____ (15). If you ever get the time, listen to a song carefully and try to _____ (16) what it is about and why it was _____ (17) – you'll probably find it interesting, too.

1	musical	music	musically	musician
2	find	was finding	will find	found
3	has been interesting	are interesting	interested	more interesting
4	goes for	goes by	goes back	goes fast
5	novel	poem	song	drama
6	thrilled	fascinated	excited	delighted
7	come	have come	came	were coming
8	actually	recently	nowadays	everyday
9	were singing	will sing	sing	was singing
10	fight	fought	fighted	fort
11	highly	higher	highest	highlier
12	innovative	psychotic	creative	chaotic
13	eventually	probably	never	always
14	expression	suppression	compression	impression
15	performances	perfomance's	performances'	performanses
16	detect	investigate	find out	examine
17	write	written	wrote	is writing

Kompetenzbereich: Sprechen (English in use) | 59

8. Give the opposite of:
   a) hot   _____
   b) bright _____
   c) night   _____
   d) up   _____
   e) fast   _____
   f) awake   _____
   g) happy   _____

9. Make the opposite of each sentence. The word that you have to change is underlined.

   a) The train is <u>late.</u>
   _____

   b) I have just <u>caught</u> the last bus home.
   _____

   c) I've <u>lost</u> my watch.
   _____

   d) He's <u>bought</u> a car.
   _____

   e) Julie's water bottle is <u>full</u>.
   _____

10. Here are five stories about people's favourite objects. Find as many synonyms as you can for each of the underlined words and write them in the grid.

    a) I've <u>only</u> won one trophy in my life and that's the reason why I still keep it. It stands on a shelf in my living room and I'm very proud of it. Sometimes I show friends my <u>greatest</u> sporting achievement.

    b) Mary says she doesn't really know why she keeps the old clown. Someone gave it to her as a present and she thought it looked happy and colourful. It sits above her telephone and smiles across the room. There's no <u>real</u> reason for keeping it – just for fun, she thinks.

    c) Jenny's first car was green – a very bright green. Her friends laughed at her when she bought it but they had a lot of fun in it, too. She took it to France one year – the poor car! <u>Many</u> years later she saw a model of it and bought it because it reminded her of all the good times she had had in it.

d) Paul can't even remember the name of his first teddy bear. He thinks it was <u>probably</u> just called Teddy. When Paul was very young he loved the teddy, chewed it and threw it around his bedroom. Poor Teddy looks <u>a bit</u> old, today, – he's actually over 50! Paul thinks it's nice to have something from when he was a child and the bear, therefore, has become a part of his home.

e) Sally's grandfather bought her a <u>famous</u> children's book when she was about seven years old. It's full of <u>beautiful</u> illustrations and exciting adventures. Sally loves the book and, of course, it reminds her of her grandfather.

Synonyms:

1	only	
2	greatest	
3	real	
4	many	
5	probably	
6	a bit	
7	famous	
8	beautiful	

11. Find synonyms which can replace the underlined words in the text. Give only <u>one</u> synonym in the grid for each of the underlined words. A synonym may consist of more than one word.

   a) I <u>like</u> music. I usually listen to rock music but I don't really mind what I hear. There are some musicians I listen to a lot but I'm not a <u>great</u> fan of anyone in particular. If the music is good, I listen to it and if it's not what I like, I don't.

   b) My friends and I <u>intend</u> to go camping in England next year. We're going to fly to Birmingham and then travel around as much as possible. I'm a little <u>worried</u> about speaking English but I'm sure that once I'm in the country it'll not be a problem.

   c) As we flew <u>across</u> the English Channel we could see a lot of small boats in the sea. We then flew over countryside before quickly <u>getting to</u> London. From the air you could see many of the sights – the Houses of Parliament, Big Ben, even Buckingham Palace. The last minutes of the journey were <u>horrible</u>, though. The pilot took the plane suddenly down to land and then I'm sure he bounced it along the runway at least five times!

   d) I <u>put on</u> my warmest clothes for my hot-air balloon trip. I was a little scared about the day but I also thought it would be fun. As I climbed into the basket I could hear the roar of the flames heating up the air. Suddenly, the balloon was fully inflated, the ropes were <u>untied</u> and we floated up into the evening sky.

e) It rained <u>the whole</u> night. No one could sleep in the tent. <u>At first</u> the noise was awful then the water <u>started</u> to drip through the tent onto our sleeping bags and clothes. Everything was wet through. As soon as it was <u>light</u> we packed up our camping equipment and went home. I've <u>hated</u> camping every since.

Synonyms:

1	like	
2	great	
3	intend	
4	worried	
5	across	
6	getting to	
7	horrible	
8	put on	
9	untied	
10	the whole	
11	at first	
12	started	
13	light	
14	hated	

12. Gib die deutschen Sätze so treffend wie möglich auf Englisch wieder. Bei dieser Aufgabe kommt es nicht darauf an, dass du die vorgegebenen Sätze wörtlich übersetzt, sondern um eine passende Wiedergabe auf Englisch.

   a) Frage deinen Freund/deine Freundin, ob er/ sie Lust hat, morgen mit dir ins Kino zu gehen

   b) Er/sie antwortet, dass er/ sie morgen leider keine Zeit hat, weil er /sie zur Chorprobe geht. Aber am Donnerstag hätte er/sie Zeit.

   c) Du sagst, dass du am Donnerstag Zeit hast. Du schlägst vor, euch um 19.30 vor dem Kino zu treffen, damit ihr rechtzeitig da seid und auch noch Karten kaufen könnt, denn der Film fängt um 20 Uhr an.

   d) Dein Freund/deine Freundin findet diese Idee gut. Er/sie freut sich auf das Treffen und verabschiedet sich.

e) Du sagst, dass du dich auch freust und verabschiedest dich auch.

13. Du telefonierst mit einer Ticketvorverkaufsstelle in London. Du möchtest Karten kaufen für dich und einen Freund für ein Konzert der Popgruppe *Dance*. Dieses Konzert möchtet ihr euch während eines Londonurlaubs ansehen. Du sprichst mit deinem Gesprächspartner Englisch.

   a) Du nennst deinen Namen und sagst, dass du dich nach Tickets für ein Konzert der Gruppe *Dance* erkundigen möchtest.

   b) Ihr möchtet gerne zum Konzert am Freitag gehen. Du möchtest wissen, wie teuer die Karten sind.

   c) Du fragst, wo der Unterschied in den verschiedenen Preiskategorien liegt, von denen der Ticketverkäufer dir erzählt.

   d) Du sagst, dass du zwei Tickets für £ 15 haben möchtest.

   e) Du fragst, ob ihr die Tickets am Tag des Konzerts beim Ticketvorverkauf abholen könnt, da ihr in Deutschland wohnt und deswegen die Tickets vorher nicht abholen könnt.

   f) Du bedankst dich für das Gespräch, verabschiedest dich höflich und wünschst noch einen schönen Tag.

14. Read the following text carefully.

Just another day

1 Henry slowly began to stir. His bed was the long corner bench of the old bus station just off Toddington's main street. He stood up, stretched his cold and aching body and began his daily routine of packing up his belongings into a few plastic bags. He usually went to the market place, found some-
5 where comfortable to sit and played a few tunes badly on his tin whistle. Once he had earned enough money he would buy his breakfast; a roll and something warm to drink.

Henry shuffled towards the High Street carrying all he owned. He didn't like people that much. They scared him. So he walked looking down at the
10 pavement investigating the empty cigarette packets and other rubbish with his tired-looking shoes as he went. After years of living on the streets Henry knew where to find things that he could use. As he turned into the main street he saw a folded piece of paper lying against the wall of the post office. He moved nearer, put his plastic bags down and bent stiffly to pick it up.
15 Money – a ten-pound note. This was enough to provide Henry with a week of breakfasts, but of course it wouldn't.

Henry woke up slowly across his usual bench in the bus station. Around him lay the empty bottles of yesterday. He was hungry. He got up, collected his things together and packed them into his bags for just another day on
20 the streets.

Which is the best dictionary meaning for each of the following words used in the text? Circle your answer.

---

stir (line 1)

stir¹ [stɜː], **stirred, stirred 1.** (um)rühren (*Suppe usw.*) **2.** (≈ *sich bewegen*) sich rühren **3.** bewegen (*Arm, Bein usw.*)

stir up [ˌstɜːrˈʌp] **1.** aufwühlen (*auch übertragen*) **2.** übertragen stiften (*Unruhe*), entfachen (*Streit*)

stir² [stɜː] **1. give something a stir** etwas (um)rühren **2. cause** (*oder* **create**) **a stir** übertragen für Aufsehen sorgen

---

comfortable (line 5)

comfortable [△ ˈkʌmftəbl] **1.** bequem; **make oneself comfortable** es sich bequem machen; **are you comfortable?** haben Sie es bequem?, sitzen *oder* liegen Sie bequem?; **feel comfortable** sich wohl fühlen **2.** *Leben usw.:* sorgenfrei **3.** *Einkommen usw.:* ausreichend, recht gut; **be comfortable** (*oder* **comfortably off**) einigermaßen wohlhabend sein

---

shuffle (line 8)

shuffle [ˈʃʌfl] **1.** mischen (*Spielkarten*) **2. shuffle (one's feet)** schlurfen

---

just (line 19)

just¹ [dʒʌst] **1.** *Person, Entscheidung:* gerecht (**to** gegen) **2.** *Strafe, Belohnung usw.:* gerecht, angemessen; **it was only just** es war nur recht und billig **3.** *Anspruch usw.:* rechtmäßig
just² [dʒʌst] **1.** *jetzt oder unmittelbar vorher:* gerade, gerade eben, (so)eben; **he's just left** er ist gerade gegangen; **just now** gerade eben, gerade jetzt; **just as** gerade als **2.** (≈ *exakt*) gerade, genau, eben; **it's just 5 o'clock** es ist genau fünf Uhr; **that's just like you** das sieht dir ähnlich **3.** gerade noch; **I arrived just in time** ich kam gerade noch pünktlich **4.** nur, lediglich, bloß; **just the three of us** nur wir drei; **just in case** für alle Fälle **5. just about** ungefähr, in etwa; **dinner's just about ready** das Essen ist so gut wie fertig

---

Abdruck mit freundlicher Genehmigung des Langenscheidt Verlags, Power Dictionary Englisch 2002

4 Kompetenzbereich: Writing

Viele Schüler sind der Meinung, dass sie sich auf den Bereich „Writing" nicht vorbereiten können, da die Aufgabenformen sehr stark variieren und die Note – wie im Deutschunterricht – ohnehin ganz von der individuellen Einschätzung des Lehrers abhänge. Erschwerend kommt im Fach Englisch noch die Fremdsprache und der damit verbundene Fehlerquotient hinzu. Aus diesen Gründen beschäftigen sich manche Schüler gar nicht erst mit dem Kompetenzbereich „Writing", was umso schlimmer ist, wenn man bedenkt, dass gerade dieser Bereich in der Regel ein Fünftel der Note in der Prüfung ausmacht.

Mache nicht den gleichen Fehler! Lies die folgenden Seiten gut durch. Du wirst sehen: Eine sinnvolle und erfolgreiche Vorbereitung auf das Schreiben kleiner Texte in Englisch ist möglich.

4.1 Strategien zum Kompetenzbereich „Writing"

Langfristige Vorbereitung

Du kannst dich auf die Writing-Aufgaben in Prüfungen nur langfristig gut vorbereiten. Wenn du dir erst zwei Tage vor der Prüfung überlegst, dass du in diesem Bereich noch Schwächen hast, dann ist das für eine sinnvolle Beschäftigung mit diesem Thema definitiv zu spät.

Schaue bzw. höre dir englischsprachige Interviews mit deinen Lieblingsstars im Fernsehen bzw. im Radio an, gehe in Kinofilme, die im englischen Originalton vorgeführt werden, schaue dir DVDs in englischer Sprache an und lies viel auf Englisch. Du wirst sehen: Mit der Zeit verstehst du immer mehr und Redewendungen kommen dir immer vertrauter vor. Eine gute Übung ist es auch, sich viel in der Fremdsprache zu unterhalten. Sprich doch hin und wieder einmal mit deinen Freunden oder deinen Geschwistern englisch. So wird dir das eigenständige Formulieren von Mal zu Mal leichter fallen.

Das Schreiben des Textes

Ganz gleich, welche Art von Texten (Briefe, E-Mails etc.) du schreiben musst, die Vorgehensweise ist dabei immer dieselbe.

Arbeitsschritt 1 Lies die Aufgabenstellung gut durch und überlege genau, was darin von dir verlangt wird. Erhältst du mit der Aufgabenstellung irgendwelche Vorgaben (z. B. Stichwörter, den Anfang oder das Ende einer Geschichte), die du in deinen Text einbringen musst? Oder sollst du einen „freien" Text schreiben?

Arbeitsschritt 2 Wenn du mehrere Themen zur Auswahl hast, dann suche dir dasjenige aus, in dem du dich am besten auskennst. Es macht keinen Sinn, einem Freund in einem Brief von den Abenteuern beim Snowboarden zu erzählen, wenn man sich mit Snowboarden gar nicht auskennt. Vermeide nach Möglichkeit also Themen, zu denen du nichts zu sagen hast.

Hast du dich für ein Thema entschieden, dann solltest du dir genau überlegen, was du dazu schreiben könntest; mache dir im Vorfeld einige Stichpunkte. Beachte dabei genau die Vorgaben aus der Aufgabenstellung (z. B. in Form von Bildern oder Stichworten) und überlege dann, was du noch hinzufügen musst. Nimm dazu ein Notizblatt. Setze dabei deiner Fantasie keine Grenzen. Eine gute Möglichkeit bietet eine Mindmap. Bei dieser Methode stellst du den zentralen Begriff, um den es bei deinem Text geht, in das Zentrum und notierst sternförmig alle weiteren Begriffe, die dir zum Thema einfallen.	Arbeitsschritt 3
Nachdem du einige Stichworte zum Thema gefunden hast, schaust du noch einmal genau auf die Aufgabenstellung und achtest darauf, dass du alle geforderten Aspekte berücksichtigst.	Arbeitsschritt 4
Nun musst du den Text formulieren. Gehe dabei Schritt für Schritt die Aufgabenstellung durch und formuliere die einzelnen Sätze aus. Achte dabei darauf, dass du Abhängigkeiten, Folgen etc. durch entsprechende Konjunktionen (Bindewörter) deutlich machst. Greife auf Redewendungen zurück, die du gelernt hast. Schreibe kurze, überschaubare Sätze; so kannst du Grammatikfehlern leichter vorbeugen. Wenn du etwas nicht ausdrücken kannst oder dir der Wortschatz fehlt, dann versuche einen anderen Aspekt zu finden. Auf den Seiten 65–67 haben wir viele Redewendungen und Phrasen zusammengestellt, die dir beim Aufsatzschreiben helfen werden. Lerne sie auswendig. Du wirst sie immer wieder einsetzen können.	Arbeitsschritt 5
Nimm dir auf jeden Fall die Zeit, am Ende alles noch einmal in Ruhe durchzulesen. Achte dabei auf die inhaltliche Geschlossenheit deines Textes. Ist alles logisch aufgebaut? Gibt es keine Gedankensprünge? Hast du die einzelnen Aspekte *(prompts)* in der Aufgabenstellung bearbeitet? Hast du die geforderten *additional aspects* nicht vergessen? Wichtig ist aber auch, dass du noch einmal gezielt nach Rechtschreib- und Grammatikfehlern suchst und diese entsprechend verbesserst. Der Inhalt wird in der Regel wesentlich höher bewertet als Rechtschreibung und Grammatik, durch einen hohen Fehlerquotienten kannst du aber trotzdem viele Punkte verlieren.	Arbeitsschritt 6

Dieses Verfahren kommt dir vielleicht ein bisschen zeitaufwändig und umständlich vor. Versuche aber dennoch einmal, genau danach vorzugehen: Du wirst bemerken, dass es dir bei den Hausaufgaben und natürlich erst recht in der Prüfung wertvolle Zeit spart. So wird es kaum passieren, dass du die falsche Aufgabe auswählst und das erst merkst, wenn du schon mitten im Schreiben bist. Klar sollte dir allerdings auch sein, dass du dieses Verfahren – das sich auch für kürzere Texte im Deutschunterricht eignet – üben musst.

TIPP

- Lies die Aufgabenstellung genau und analysiere sie.
- Wähle die für dich geeignete Aufgabe aus.
- Mache dir einige Stichpunkte.
- Überprüfe, ob du alle Aspekte der Aufgabenstellung berücksichtigt hast.
- Formuliere den Text anhand der Aufgabenstellung und der vorgegebenen *prompts* Schritt für Schritt aus.
- Lies deinen Text abschließend noch einmal genau durch und überprüfe dabei, ob alles logisch aufgebaut und verständlich geschrieben ist. Verbessere Rechtschreib- und Grammatikfehler.

4.2 Hilfreiche Wendungen zum Kompetenzbereich „Writing"

Anrede und Schlussformeln

Persönlicher Brief

Liebe Jane,	Dear Jane,
Viele Grüße / Liebe Grüße	Best wishes
	Love *(nur bei sehr guten Freunden, aber nicht unter Männern)*

Geschäftsbrief / Anfrage

wenn du den Namen des Ansprechpartners nicht kennst

Sehr geehrte Damen und Herren,	Dear Sir / Madam,
Mit freundlichen Grüßen	Yours faithfully

wenn du den Namen des Ansprechpartners kennst

Sehr geehrte Frau Roberts,	Dear Mrs Roberts,
Sehr geehrter Herr James,	Dear Mr James,
wenn du nicht weißt, ob die Frau verheiratet ist oder nicht	Dear Ms Bell,
Mit freundlichen Grüßen	Yours sincerely

Einleitung und Schluss des Briefes

Danke für …	Thank you for …
Ich habe … erhalten.	I received …
Ich hoffe, dass …	I hope that …
Wie geht es dir?	How are you?
Im letzten Brief hast du mir von … erzählt.	In your last letter you told me about …
Im letzten Brief hast du mir erzählt, dass …	In your last letter you told me that …

Entschuldige, dass ich … vergessen habe, aber …	Sorry that I forgot to …, but …
Sage bitte … / Richte … bitte aus	Please tell …
Es wäre schön, wenn wir uns treffen könnten.	It would be nice if we could meet.
Bitte richte … Grüße aus.	Best wishes to … (Please) give my regards to …
Bitte schreibe mir bald zurück.	Write soon.
Ich freue mich darauf, bald von dir zu hören.	I'm looking forward to hearing from you. I hope I'll hear from you soon.
Ich freue mich auf deinen Brief.	I'm looking forward to your letter.
Ich werde dich anrufen.	I'll call you.

Häufig vorkommende Redewendungen / Ausdrücke

sich entschuldigen	I'm sorry
etwas bedauern	It's a pity that … / I'm disappointed that …
an etwas erinnern	Please remember to …
Überraschung äußern	I was surprised that …
eine Bitte äußern	Could you / Would you …, please?
einen Wunsch äußern	I'd like to …
einen Entschluss mitteilen	I've decided to … I've made up my mind to … I'm going to …
eine Absicht mitteilen	I intend to / I'm planning to … I want to / I will …
Interesse ausdrücken	I'm interested in …
Freude ausdrücken	I'm happy/glad about
Überzeugung ausdrücken	I'm convinced that … I'm sure that …
nach dem Preis fragen	How much is it? / How much does it cost?
Ich hoffe, dir hat … gefallen.	I hope you liked/enjoyed …
Ich muss jetzt …	I have to …
Ich denke, es ist besser …	I think it's better to …

Auskunft geben über sich selbst

Ich wohne in …	I live in …
Ich wurde am … in … geboren.	I was born on (17th August, 1992) in …

Ich interessiere mich für ...	I'm interested in ...
Ich war schon in ...	I've (already) been in .../to ...
Ich möchte gerne ... werden.	I'd like to be a/an ...
Mir geht es gut.	I'm fine.
Mir geht es nicht gut.	I'm not well.
Ich mag ...	I like ... / I enjoy ...
Ich mag ... lieber (als ...).	I prefer to ... / I like ... better (than ...)
Ich weiß ... noch nicht genau.	I still don't know exactly.
Ich plane, ... zu tun.	I plan to ...
Ich freue mich (sehr) auf ...	I'm looking forward to ... I'm excited about ...
Ich konnte ... nicht ...	I wasn't able to ... / I couldn't ...
In meiner Freizeit ...	In my free time/spare time ...
Ich nehme regelmäßig an ... teil.	I take part in ...

Layout eines Geschäftsbriefes

```
                                    24 Castle Street      ⎫
                                    Blackburn             ⎬  writer's address
                                    Lancashire            ⎭
                                    LK6 5TQ

                                    6th March 2006           date

Mrs J. Fox                                                ⎫
Dane Cleaners                                             ⎪  recipient's name
3 Arthur Road                                             ⎬  and address
Doddington                                                ⎪  (formal letters only)
NE3 6LD                                                   ⎭


Dear Mrs Fox,                                                salutation

Thank you for your letter ...                                letter




Yours sincerely,                                             closing
Adam Smith                                                   signature
Adam Smith                                                   name
```

4.3 Häufige Aufgabenstellungen zum Kompetenzbereich „Writing"

Bildimpulse

Häufig werden dir Bilder als visuelle Impulse vorgegeben. Dann sollst du das Bild (oder die Bilder) lediglich als „Aufhänger" für eine kleine Geschichte benutzen. In diesem Fall empfiehlt es sich, das Bild/die Bilder zuerst einmal genau zu betrachten. Eine intensive Bildbeschreibung ist allerdings selten nötig, du sollst vielmehr deiner Fantasie freien Lauf lassen.

Dialoge

Das Abfassen von Dialogen erfordert sehr viel Kreativität. Bei solchen Aufgaben musst du dir zunächst einmal ganz genau überlegen, **wen** du sprechen lassen sollst. Ein Dialog muss immer „echt" wirken. Wenn du in deinem Dialog beispielsweise zwei Schüler miteinander sprechen lässt, solltest du versuchen, Jugendsprache einfließen zu lassen. Außerdem sind dann eher Kurzformen statt Langformen einzusetzen (z. B. „I'd ..." statt „I would ...").

Briefe und E-Mails

Natürlich ist auch die Bandbreite an Aufgaben zum Verfassen von Briefen und E-Mails groß. Dabei können sowohl formelle als auch persönliche Briefe oder E-Mails verlangt sein.

- **Formelle** Briefe und E-Mails: Achte darauf, dass du keine saloppen Ausdrücke und Formulierungen verwendest. Bleibe in deiner Ausdrucksweise sachlich und nüchtern.
- **Persönliche** Briefe und E-Mails: Wie beim Schreiben von Dialogen solltest du bei persönlichen Briefen oder E-Mails zunächst einmal überlegen, in welche Rolle du schlüpfen sollst. Meist musst du als „fiktive", d. h. erfundene Person einem fiktiven Freund einen Brief schreiben und ihn über bestimmte Geschehnisse informieren. Dabei müssen Sprache und Stil des Briefes natürlich zu der Person passen, in deren Namen du den Brief oder die E-Mail verfasst.

Guided writing

Bei diesen Aufgabenformen werden dir immer Vorgaben gemacht, die du in deinen Text einbauen kannst oder manchmal sogar musst. Es handelt sich hierbei also um ein „gelenktes" Schreiben. Die Vorgaben können ganz unterschiedlich ausfallen: Manchmal werden **Stichwörter** (Reizwörter) angegeben, manchmal werden dir **Bilder** vorgelegt, manchmal erhältst du eine Kombination aus verschiedenen Vorgaben. Ob du auf die Vorgaben eingehen musst oder nicht, steht in der Aufgabenstellung.

Comment

In diesen Aufgaben wirst du aufgefordert, einen freien Text zu verfassen, ohne dass dir Vorgaben z. B. in Form von Stichworten gemacht werden. Hier ist deine Kreativität gefragt. Manchmal erhältst du nur einfach ein Thema und dieses sollst du dann in deinem kleinen Aufsatz diskutieren. Bei dieser Aufgabe ist es wichtig, dass du die Aufgabenstellung sorgfältig liest und dir genau überlegst, was hier von dir verlangt wird. Es ist eine Anzahl von Wörtern vorgegeben, die dein Text ungefähr umfassen sollte.

4.4 Übungsaufgaben zum Kompetenzbreich „Writing"

1. Make the following sentences better. You are given words which you can use: horror, dirty, loud, long, summer, old, terrible.

   a) The _____ house was at the end of the street.

   b) Jane likes listening to _____ music in her bedroom.

   c) The _____ boy ran away.

   d) We had a _____ meal in the restaurant.

   e) I didn't like the _____ film it was boring.

   f) My _____ holiday was great.

   g) There was a _____ beach with no one on it.

2. Look at the photograph. What can you say about it?

   a) Where is the police car?
   _____

   b) What is behind the police car?
   _____

c) Who is standing next to the police car?

d) Describe the police car.

e) Describe the policewoman's uniform.

3. Look at your answers to question 2. Make each answer better by adding more information – an adverb or an adjective.

   a) Where is the car?
      (Answer in question 2) The police car is in a village.
      The police car is in a small village.

   b)

   c)

   d)

   e)

4. Using the photograph write a small text (about 50 words) to a friend. Say that you saw an English police car and give information about the English police. Use the past tense.
   ▶ *Schreibe, wo du das Polizeiauto gesehen hast.*
   ▶ *Beschreibe das Auto.*
   ▶ *Schreibe über die Polizei.*
   ▶ *Hier sind einige Ausdrücke, die du vielleicht brauchst:*
      a bulletproof jacket, fluorescent jacket

5. Picture story with guided notes. Write about 50–100 words. Try to describe things well. Use the past tense.
   - parking the car
   - getting to the castle wall
   - sign
   - tired
   - getting to the entrance of the castle
   - sign
   - going back to the car
   - tired and angry

If you need help starting, you can use this first sentence:
In the morning we drove two hours to Bury Castle.

Kompetenzbereich: Writing | 73

6. Look at the longer picture story. Read the notes you are given and then make more if you can. Write about 130 words using the picture story. Use the past tense.

a robbery in 1965
notes: an art robbery
small picture by van Gogh

_____
_____
_____
_____
_____

Mr Smith in his garden
notes:

_____
_____
_____
_____
_____

finds a packet
notes:

_____
_____
_____
_____
_____

phones art gallery
notes:

_____
_____
_____
_____
_____
_____

gives picture to gallery
notes:

_____
_____
_____
_____
_____

a reward
notes:

_____
_____
_____
_____
_____

7. What would you say? Make each answer longer so that it is like a conversation. Think carefully about the situation.
   For example: "Do you like watching television?"
                 "No, I don't. I like reading books."

   a) "Hello, my name is Paul."
   _____
   _____

   b) (in a flower shop) "Can I help you?"
   _____
   _____

   c) "Could you tell me the time, please?"
   _____
   _____

   d) "What is English like in your school?"
   _____
   _____

   e) "Do you like playing football?"
   _____
   _____

8. What is the right start and ending for each of these letters? You are writing to:

   a) John, a friend

   b) someone at a bank

   c) a woman named Peterson

   d) Mrs Fiona Black

   e) a woman in a shop

   f) Mike Petty in a travel agent's

   g) your penfriend (Wendy Blue)

   h) a man in an office

9. Put the information below into a good letter layout.
   (Achte auf Groß- und Kleinschreibung und auch auf die Zeichensetzung.)

   yesterday, I saw your advertisement in the newspaper for ...
   6/8/06
   John Stuart
   dear
   sir / madam
   yours faithfully
   31 Appletree Lane, Norwich, PE67 2ST
   (for) Computer City, 19 Park Road, Bath, BR2 7FD

Kompetenzbereich: Writing

Kompetenzbereich: Writing | 77

10. You are an old person living in this street. You are angry because people park their cars on the pavement and you cannot walk past them. Write to the mayor about this problem. Complete the missing parts of the letter with the information from the question and the notes.

   ▶ *Vergiss nicht deine Adresse, das Datum und die Anrede.*
   ▶ *Schreibe, wer du bist.*
   ▶ *Schreibe, wo du wohnst.*
   ▶ *Gib an, warum du schreibst.*
   ▶ *Erkläre das Problem.*
   ▶ *Kinder/Gefahr*
   ▶ *Frage, ob man das Parken verbieten kann.*
   ▶ *höflicher Schluss/Kann man etwas tun?*
   ▶ *Briefschluss*

_____
_____
_____
_____

_____

_____
I am an _____ who lives in _____. I am _____ to you because of the parked _____.
The drivers park their cars _____ and no one can _____ past them. You always have to walk _____.
This is also not very nice for _____. It is very _____? I hope that you _____.

_____
_____
_____

Kompetenzbereich: Writing

11. Write to a friend. Tell him/her about the street musicians that you saw in Cambridge. Use the notes to help you.

    - *Adresse, Datum, Anrede*
    - *freundlicher erster Satz/Frage, wie es ihm/ihr geht*
    - *In Cambridge sahst du Musiker (street musicians)./Wo?*
    - *Sie spielten gute Musik./ Es machte Spaß, ihnen zuzuschauen.*
    - *Sie brachten einen kleinen Jungen dazu, mit ihnen zu spielen.*
    - *lustig*
    - *Sie verkauften (sell) CDs./zehn Pfund*
    - *Du hast keine gekauft (buy)./kein Geld*
    - *Du hast ihnen lange zugeschaut./sehr gut*
    - *Du hast Fotos gemacht.*
    - *Du zeigst (show) sie ihm/ihr nächste Woche.*
    - *bis bald*
    - *Briefschluss*

12. You see an advert in a newspaper, The Daily News, for a holiday in Great Britain and you want more information. Write about 10 sentences using the advert and the information. This is a formal letter.

> Fly to Great Britain:
>
> # London for only £45
>
> Hotel + breakfast
> Rooms: single and double
> City tours possible
>
> Contact: Mike Johnson, BritHols, 36 Luton Road, Bedford, BD9 RT5

Start the letter correctly. Where did you see the advert? Explain that you are interested in going to London. You want to know where the hotel is. Say when you want to go and what type of room you need. Ask about meals. Find out about the city tour and the price. End the letter.

13. You see an advert for a job in England for one year. You want to write an e-mail and get more information about it. Read the advert carefully and follow the notes.

Farmlands

Busy holiday centre in Scotland
offers students a 12-month work experience

accommodation – meals – all types of work

Details & e-mail: LucyMacdonald@Farmlands.uk

- Where?
- How much must I pay?
- What must I do?

▸ work: hours / days?
▸ holidays?
▸ pay?
▸ about myself: name / where I come from / why I would like the job

14. You get a job at Farmlands (exercise 13). Two weeks before you go to Scotland Lucy sends you an e-mail. Answer it.

working details - Nachricht (Rich-Text)

An: Lena <Stark@mail.de>
Von: Lucy <Macdonald@Farmlands.uk>
Betreff: working details

Do you know when and where you arrive in Scotland? The nearest airport is at Glasgow. You can get a train from Glasgow to Aberdeen or I can meet you at the airport. I forgot to ask you, do you eat everything or are there some things that you do not like? At Farmlands we like to use our first names, so please call me Lucy.

Best wishes,
Lucy

15. Comment

    About **travel:** Choose one of the following tasks and write at least 150 words.

    a) Where in the world would you like to visit? Why do you want to go there?

    b) What method(s) of travelling do you prefer? Which methods don't you like (or do not appeal to you)? Explain your reasons clearly.

16. Comment

    About **free time**: Choose one of the following tasks and write at least 150 words.

    a) Young people are often criticised for just sitting in front of a television or a computer screen. How do you react to this?

    b) What would you like to do in your free time that you do not already do? Explain why you have not done this yet.

17. Comment

    About **work:** Choose one of the following tasks and write at least 150 words.

    a) Apart from qualifications what else do you think is important when you are trying to get a job? (Think particularly about first impressions.)

    b) As a young person, would you move far away from home to take a job? Give your opinion about this.

▶ **Kurzgrammatik**

Anhang: Kurzgrammatik zum schnellen Nachschlagen und Auffinden

Der Bereich Grammatik ist zwar wenig beliebt aber dennoch ganz elementar für das Lernen und Anwenden einer Sprache: Ganz gleich, ob du dich in einer Sprache passiv (d. h. jemandem zuhören oder etwas lesen) oder aktiv (d. h. selbst sprechen oder schreiben) verständigen möchtest, immer ist es wichtig, dass du die verwendeten Satzkonstruktionen verstehst und selbst anwenden kannst. Wenn du beispielsweise die Zeitformen nicht beherrschst, wird es dir recht schwer fallen, einer Person begreiflich zu machen, ob das, was du ihr sagst, vergangen ist, jetzt stattfindet oder erst morgen oder übermorgen stattfinden wird. Auch wenn Grammatik kein direkter Teil deiner Abschlussprüfung ist, musst du sie dennoch in all deinen Prüfungsteilen beherrschen: du musst grammatikalisch korrekte Sätze bilden oder bestimmte grammatikalische Formen erkennen, um die richtige Form in den Lückentext einsetzen zu können. Deine Grammatikkenntnisse werden also indirekt in allen Kompetenzbereichen geprüft.

Aus diesem Grund haben wir für dich die wichtigsten Grammatikregeln übersichtlich zusammengestellt. In der linken Spalte findest du die Regeln, in der rechten Spalte kannst du die entsprechenden Beispiele dazu ansehen.

1 Adverbien – *adverbs*

Bildung		
Adjektiv + *-ly*	glad	→ gladly
Ausnahmen:		
• -y am Wortende wird zu -i	easy	→ easily
	funny	→ funnily
• auf einen Konsonanten folgendes -le wird zu -ly	simple	→ simply
	horrible	→ horribly
	probable	→ probably
• auf einen Konsonanten folgendes -ic wird zu -ically	fantastic	→ fantastically
Ausnahme:	public	→ publicly

Beachte:
- In einigen Fällen haben Adjektiv und Adverb dieselbe Form.
- Unregelmäßig gebildet wird:
- Endet das Adjektiv auf -ly, so kannst du kein Adverb bilden und verwendest deshalb: *in a* + Adjektiv + *manner*

daily, early, fast, hard, long, low, weekly, yearly

good → well

friendly → in a friendly manner

Verwendung

Adverbien bestimmen

- Verben,

She <u>easily</u> <u>found</u> her brother in the crowd.
Sie <u>fand</u> ihren Bruder <u>leicht</u> in der Menge.

- Adjektive oder

This band is <u>extremely</u> <u>famous</u>.
Diese Band ist <u>sehr</u> <u>berühmt</u>.

- andere Adverbien näher.

He walks <u>extremely</u> <u>quickly</u>.
Er geht <u>äußerst</u> <u>schnell</u>.

2 Bedingungssätze – *if-clauses*

Ein Bedingungssatz besteht aus zwei Teilen: Nebensatz (*if*-Satz) + Hauptsatz. Im **if-Satz** steht die **Bedingung**, unter der die im **Hauptsatz** genannte **Folge** eintritt. Man unterscheidet drei Hauptarten von Bedingungssätzen.

Bedingungssatz Typ I

Bildung
- *if*-Satz (Bedingung): Gegenwart (*simple present*)
- Hauptsatz (Folge): Zukunft mit *will* (*will-future*)

If you <u>read</u> this book,
Wenn du dieses Buch liest,

you <u>will learn</u> a lot about Scotland.
erfährst du eine Menge über Schottland.

Der *if*-Satz kann auch nach dem Hauptsatz stehen:
- Hauptsatz: *will-future*

You <u>will learn</u> a lot about Scotland,
Du erfährst eine Menge über Schottland,

- *if*-Satz: *simple present*

<u>if</u> you <u>read</u> this book.
wenn du dieses Buch liest.

Im Hauptsatz kann statt *will-future* auch
- *can* + Grundform des Verbs oder

If you go to London, you <u>can see</u> Sandy.
Wenn du nach London gehst, kannst du Sandy treffen.

- *must* + Grundform des Verbs stehen.

If you go to London, you <u>must visit</u> Big Ben.
Wenn du nach London gehst, musst du dir Big Ben ansehen.

Verwendung

Bedingungssätze vom Typ I verwendet man, wenn die **Bedingung erfüllbar** ist. Man gibt an, was unter bestimmten Bedingungen **geschieht, geschehen kann** oder was **geschehen sollte**.

If it's hot, we will go to the beach.
Wenn es heiß ist, gehen wir an den Strand.

If it's hot, we can go to the beach.
Wenn es heiß ist, können wir an den Strand gehen.

If it's hot, we must go to the beach.
Wenn es heiß ist, müssen wir an den Strand gehen.

Sonderform

Bedingungssätze vom Typ I verwendet man auch bei einer generellen Regel *(automatic result)*. Hierbei steht sowohl im Hauptsatz als auch im *if*-Satz das *simple present*.

If you add blue to yellow you get green.
Wenn du die Farbe Blau zu Gelb dazugibst, erhältst zu Grün.

Bedingungssatz Typ II

Bildung

- *if*-Satz (Bedingung):
  1.Vergangenheit *(simple past)*
- Hauptsatz (Folge): Konditional I
  (conditional I = would + Grundform des Verbs)

If I went to London,
Wenn ich nach London ginge/gehen würde,

I would visit the Tower of London.
würde ich mir den Tower of London ansehen.

Verwendung

Bedingungssätze vom Typ II verwendet man, wenn die **Erfüllung der Bedingung unwahrscheinlich** ist.

Bedingungssatz Typ III

Bildung

- *if*-Satz (Bedingung):
  Vorvergangenheit *(past perfect)*
- Hauptsatz (Folge): Konditional II
  (conditional II)

If I had gone to London,
Wenn ich nach London gegangen wäre,

I would have visited the Tower of London.
hätte ich mir den Tower of London angesehen.

Verwendung

Bedingungssätze vom Typ III verwendet man, wenn sich die **Bedingung auf die Vergangenheit bezieht** und deshalb **nicht mehr erfüllbar** ist.

3 Fürwörter – *pronouns*

Besitzanzeigende Fürwörter – *possessive pronouns*

Besitzanzeigende Fürwörter *(possessive pronouns)* verwendet man, um zu sagen, **was (zu) jemandem gehört**.
Die Formen der besitzanzeigenden Fürwörter unterscheiden sich je nachdem, ob sie alleine oder bei einem Substantiv stehen:

mit Substantiv	ohne Substantiv
my	mine
your	yours
his/her/its	his/hers/its
our	ours
your	yours
their	theirs

This is my bike. – This is mine.
This is your bike. – This is yours.
This is her bike. – This is hers.
This is our bike. – This is ours.
This is your bike. – This is yours.
This is their bike. – This is theirs

Rückbezügliche Fürwörter – *reflexive pronouns*

Die rückbezüglichen Fürwörter *(reflexive pronouns)* **beziehen sich auf das Subjekt** des Satzes **zurück**:

myself	I will buy myself a new car.
yourself	You will buy yourself a new car.
himself/herself/itself	He will buy himself a new car.
ourselves	We will buy ourselves a new car.
yourselves	You will buy yourselves a new car.
themselves	They will buy themselves a new car.

each other / one another

each other / one another ist unveränderlich. Es bezieht sich auf **mehrere Personen** und wird mit „sich (gegenseitig), einander" übersetzt.

They looked at each other and laughed.
Sie schauten sich (gegenseitig) an und lachten.
oder: *Sie schauten einander an und lachten.*

Beachte:
Einige Verben stehen ohne *each other*, obwohl sie im Deutschen mit „sich" verbunden werden.

to meet	sich treffen
to kiss	sich küssen
to fall in love	sich verlieben

4 Grundform – *infinitive*

Die Grundform mit *to* steht nach

- bestimmten Verben, z. B.:

(to) agree	zustimmen
(to) attempt	versuchen
(to) choose	wählen
(to) decide	entscheiden
(to) expect	erwarten
(to) forget	vergessen
(to) hope	hoffen
(to) manage	schaffen
(to) offer	anbieten
(to) plan	planen
(to) promise	versprechen
(to) remember	an etw. denken
(to) seem	scheinen
(to) try	versuchen
(to) want	wollen

He <u>decided</u> <u>to wait</u>.
Er beschloss zu warten.

- bestimmten Substantiven, z. B.:

attempt	Versuch
idea	Idee
plan	Plan
wish	Wunsch

It was her <u>wish</u> <u>to marry</u> in November.
Es war ihr Wunsch, im November zu heiraten.

- bestimmten Adjektiven, z. B.:

certain	sicher
difficult	schwer, schwierig
easy	leicht
hard	schwer, schwierig

It was <u>difficult</u> <u>to follow</u> her.
Es war schwierig, ihr zu folgen.

- den Fragewörtern *what, where, which, who, when, why, how*.

We knew <u>where</u> <u>to find</u> her.
Wir wussten, wo wir sie finden würden.

5 Indirekte Rede – *reported speech*

Die indirekte Rede verwendet man, um **wiederzugeben, was ein anderer gesagt** oder **gefragt hat**.

Bildung

Um die indirekte Rede zu bilden, benötigt man ein **Einleitungsverb**. Häufig verwendete Einleitungsverben sind:

to **add**, to **agree**, to **answer**, to **ask**, to **say**, to **tell**, to **think**, to **want to know**

In der indirekten Rede verändern sich die **Fürwörter**, in bestimmten Fällen auch die **Zeiten** und die **Orts-** und **Zeitangaben**.

- Veränderung der **Fürwörter**
  persönliche Fürwörter:
  besitzanzeigende Fürwörter:
  hinweisende Fürwörter:

direkte Rede:	indirekte Rede:
I, you, we, you	he, she, they
my, your, our, your	his, her, their
this, these	that, those

- **Zeiten**
  Keine Veränderung, wenn das **Einleitungsverb** in der **Gegenwart**, der **2. Vergangenheit** (Perfekt) oder der **Zukunft** steht.

direkte Rede:	indirekte Rede:
Jill <u>says</u>, "I <u>love</u> dancing."	Jill <u>says</u> (that) she <u>loves</u> dancing.
Jill sagt: „Ich tanze sehr gerne."	Jill sagt, sie tanzt sehr gerne.

Die Zeit der direkten Rede wird in der indirekten Rede **um eine Zeitstufe zurückversetzt**, wenn das **Einleitungsverb** in der **1. Vergangenheit** steht. Die Zeiten verändern sich dann folgendermaßen:

Jill <u>said</u>, "I <u>love</u> dancing."	Jill <u>said</u> (that) she <u>loved</u> dancing.
Jill sagte: „Ich tanze sehr gerne."	Jill sagte, sie tanze sehr gerne.

direkte Rede		indirekte Rede
simple present	→	simple past
simple past	→	past perfect
present perfect	→	past perfect
will-future	→	conditional I

Joe: "I <u>like</u> it."	Joe said he <u>liked</u> it.
Joe: "I <u>liked</u> it."	Joe said he <u>had liked</u> it.
Joe: "I've <u>liked</u> it."	Joe said he <u>had liked</u> it.
Joe: "I <u>will like</u> it."	Joe said he <u>would like</u> it.

- Veränderung der **Orts-** und **Zeitangaben**:

now	→	then
today	→	that day
yesterday	→	the day before
the day before yesterday	→	two days before
tomorrow	→	the next day
next week/year	→	the following week/year
here	→	there

Bildung der indirekten Frage
Häufige Einleitungsverben für die indirekte Frage sind *to ask, to want to know*.

- Enthält die direkte Frage ein **Fragewort**, **bleibt** dieses in der indirekten Frage **erhalten**. Die **Umschreibung** mit *do/does/did* **entfällt** in der indirekten Frage.

Tom: "<u>When</u> did they arrive in England?"	Tom asked <u>when</u> they had arrived in England.
Tom: „Wann sind sie in England angekommen?"	Tom fragte, wann sie in England angekommen seien.

- Enthält die direkte Frage **kein Fragewort**, wird die indirekte Frage mit **whether** oder **if** eingeleitet:

Tom: "Are they staying at the youth hostel?"	Tom asked <u>if/whether</u> they were staying at the youth hostel.
Tom: „Übernachten sie in der Jugendherberge?"	Tom fragte, ob sie in der Jugendherberge übernachteten.

Befehle/Aufforderungen in der indirekten Rede

Häufige Einleitungsverben sind *to tell*, *to order* (Befehl), *to ask* (Aufforderung). In der indirekten Rede steht bei Befehlen/Aufforderungen **Einleitungsverb + Objekt + (not) to + Grundform des Verbs** der direkten Rede.

Tom: "Leave the room."
Tom: „Verlass den Raum."

Tom told me to leave the room.
Tom forderte mich auf, den Raum zu verlassen.

6 Modale Hilfsverben – *modal auxiliaries*

Im Englischen gibt es zwei Arten von Hilfsverben: die vollständigen Hilfsverben *to be, to have, to do* und die **modalen Hilfsverben** (*modal auxiliaries*) *can, may, must, shall, will*.

Bildung

- Die modalen Hilfsverben haben für alle Personen **nur eine Form**, in der 3. Person Singular also kein -s.

  I, you, he/she/it, we, you, they } must

- Auf das modale Hilfsverb folgt die **Grundform** des Verbs **ohne *to***.

  You must listen to my new CD.
  Du musst dir meine neue CD anhören.

- **Frage und Verneinung** werden **nicht** mit *do/does/did* umschrieben.

  Can I have a cup of coffee, please?
  Kann ich bitte eine Tasse Kaffee haben?

Die modalen Hilfsverben können nicht alle Zeiten bilden. Deshalb benötigt man bestimmte **Ersatzformen**.

- **can** (können)
  simple past/conditional I: *could*
  Ersatzform: *to be able to*

  I can sing. / I will be able to sing.
  Ich kann singen. / Ich werde singen können.

- **may** (dürfen)
  conditional: *might*
  Ersatzform: *to be allowed to*

  You may go home early today. /
  You were allowed to go home early yesterday.
  Du darfst heute früh nach Hause gehen. /
  Du durftest gestern früh nach Hause gehen.

- **must** (müssen)
  Ersatzform: *to have to*

  He must be home by ten o'clock. /
  He had to be home by ten o'clock.
  Er muss um zehn Uhr zu Hause sein. /
  Er musste um zehn Uhr zu Hause sein.

Beachte:
must not/mustn't = nicht dürfen

You must not eat all the cake.
Du darfst nicht den ganzen Kuchen essen.

nicht müssen = *not + to have to*

You don't have to eat all the cake.
Du musst nicht den ganzen Kuchen essen.

- **shall** (sollen)
  conditional I: **should**
  Ersatzform: *to be to, to want*

  Shall I help you? / Do you want me to help you?
  Soll ich dir helfen?

7 Konjunktionen – *conjunctions*

> Konjunktionen *(conjunctions)* verwendet man, um **zwei Hauptsätze oder Haupt- und Nebensatz miteinander zu verbinden**. Mit Konjunktionen lässt sich ein Text strukturieren, indem man z. B. Ursachen, Folgen oder zeitliche Abfolgen angibt.

English	Deutsch	Beispiel
after	nachdem	What will you do <u>after</u> she's gone? *Was wirst du tun, <u>nachdem</u> sie gegangen ist?*
although	obwohl	<u>Although</u> she was ill, she went to work. *<u>Obwohl</u> sie krank war, ging sie zur Arbeit.*
as	als (zeitlich)	<u>As</u> he came into the room, the telephone rang. *<u>Als</u> er ins Zimmer kam, klingelte das Telefon.*
as soon as	sobald	<u>As soon as</u> the band began to play, … *<u>Sobald</u> die Band zu spielen begann, …*
because	weil, da	I need a new bike <u>because</u> my old bike was stolen. *Ich brauche ein neues Rad, <u>weil</u> mein altes Rad gestohlen wurde.*
before	bevor	<u>Before</u> he goes to work, he buys a newspaper. *<u>Bevor</u> er zur Arbeit geht, kauft er eine Zeitung.*
but	aber	She likes football <u>but</u> she doesn't like skiing. *Sie mag Fußball, <u>aber</u> sie mag Skifahren nicht.*
either … or	entweder … oder	We can <u>either</u> watch a film <u>or</u> go to a concert. *Wir können uns <u>entweder</u> einen Film ansehen <u>oder</u> in ein Konzert gehen.*
in order to	um … zu, damit	Peter is in Scotland <u>in order to</u> visit his friend Malcolm. *Peter ist in Schottland, <u>um</u> seinen Freund Malcolm <u>zu</u> besuchen.*
neither … nor	weder … noch	We can <u>neither</u> eat <u>nor</u> sleep outside. It's raining. *Wir können <u>weder</u> draußen essen <u>noch</u> draußen schlafen. Es regnet.*
so that	sodass	She shut the door <u>so that</u> the dog couldn't go outside. *Sie machte die Tür zu, <u>sodass</u> der Hund nicht hinausgehen konnte.*
then	dann	He bought an ice cream, and <u>then</u> shared it with Sally. *Er kaufte ein Eis, (und) <u>dann</u> teilte er es mit Sally.*
when	wenn (zeitlich), sobald	Have a break <u>when</u> you've finished painting this wall. *Mach eine Pause, <u>sobald</u> du diese Wand fertig gestrichen hast.*

Kurzgrammatik zum schnellen Nachschlagen und Auffinden

while	– während, solange

While we were in London, we had very good weather.
Während wir in London waren, hatten wir sehr gutes Wetter.

8 Partizipien – *participles*

Partizip Präsens – *present participle*

Bildung

Grundform des Verbs + *-ing*

read → read**ing**

Beachte:

- stumm**e**s *-e* entfällt

  writ**e** → writing

- nach kurzem betonten Vokal wird der Schlusskonsonant verdoppelt

  sto**p** → sto**pp**ing

- *-ie* wird zu *-y*

  l**ie** → l**y**ing

Verwendung

Das Partizip Präsens *(present participle)* verwendet man

- zur Bildung der Verlaufsform der Gegenwart,

  Peter is reading.
  Peter liest (gerade).

- zur Bildung der Verlaufsform der Vergangenheit,

  Peter was reading when I came into the room.
  Peter las (gerade), als ich in den Raum kam.

- zur Verkürzung eines Nebensatzes oder zur Verbindung von zwei Hauptsätzen mit demselben Subjekt (siehe S. 92/93).

Partizip Perfekt – *past participle*

Bildung

Grundform des Verbs + *-ed*

talk → talk**ed**

Beachte:

- stumm**e**s *-e* entfällt

  liv**e** → liv**ed**

- nach kurzem betonten Vokal wird der Schlusskonsonant verdoppelt

  sto**p** → sto**pp**ed

- *-y* wird zu *-ie*

  cr**y** → cr**ied**

- unregelmäßige Verben: siehe die Liste in deinem Schulbuch. Die *past-participle*-Formen einiger wichtiger unregelmäßiger Verben sind hier angegeben.

  be → been
  have → had
  give → given
  go → gone
  meet → met
  say → said

Verwendung

Das Partizip Perfekt *(past participle)* verwendet man

- zur Bildung der zweiten Vergangenheit *(present perfect)*,

  He has <u>talked</u> to his father.
  Er hat mit seinem Vater gesprochen.

- zur Bildung der Vorvergangenheit *(past perfect)*,

  Before they went cycling in France they had <u>bought</u> new bicycles.
  Bevor sie nach Frankreich zum Radfahren gingen, hatten sie neue Fahrräder gekauft.

- zur Bildung des Passivs,

  The fish was <u>eaten</u> by the cat.
  Der Fisch wurde von der Katze gegessen.

- zur Verkürzung eines Nebensatzes oder zur Verbindung von zwei Hauptsätzen mit demselben Subjekt.

Verkürzung eines Nebensatzes durch ein Partizip

Kausal-, Temporal- oder **Relativsätze** können durch ein Partizip verkürzt werden, wenn **Haupt- und Nebensatz dasselbe Subjekt** haben. Aus der Zeitform des Verbs im Nebensatz ergibt sich, ob das **Partizip Präsens** oder das **Partizip Perfekt** für die Satzverkürzung verwendet wird:

<u>She</u> watches the news, because <u>she</u> wants to stay informed.
Sie sieht sich die Nachrichten an, weil sie informiert bleiben möchte.

<u>Wanting</u> to stay informed, she watches the news.
Weil sie informiert bleiben möchte, sieht sie sich die Nachrichten an.

- Steht das Verb im Nebensatz im *simple present* oder im *simple past*, verwendet man das Partizip Präsens.

  he finishes / he finished → finishing

- Steht das Verb im Nebensatz im *present perfect* oder im *past perfect*, verwendet man *having* + Partizip Perfekt.

  he has finished / he had finished → having finished

Beachte:

- Bei **Kausalsätzen** entfallen die Konjunktionen *as, because, since* im verkürzten Nebensatz.

  As <u>he</u> was hungry, <u>he</u> bought a sandwich.
  <u>Being</u> hungry, he bought a sandwich.
  Da er hungrig war, kaufte er ein Sandwich.

- Bei **Temporalsätzen** bleiben die Konjunktionen *when, while, before* im verkürzten Nebensatz erhalten; *after* kann entfallen.

  After <u>he</u> had finished breakfast, <u>he</u> went to work.
  After having finished / Having finished breakfast, he went to work.
  Nachdem er sein Frühstück beendet hatte, ging er zur Arbeit.

  When <u>he</u> left, <u>he</u> forgot to lock the door.
  When leaving, he forgot to lock the door.
  Als er ging, vergaß er, die Tür abzuschließen.

- Bei **Relativsätzen** entfallen die Relativpronomen *who, which*.

I saw a six-year-old boy who played the piano.
I saw a six-year-old boy playing the piano.
Ich habe einen sechsjährigen Jungen gesehen, der Klavier spielte. / Ich habe einen sechsjährigen Jungen Klavier spielen sehen.

Verbindung von zwei Hauptsätzen durch ein Partizip

Zwei Hauptsätze können durch ein Partizip zu einem Hauptsatz verbunden werden, wenn sie **dasselbe Subjekt** haben.

Beachte:
- Das Subjekt des zweiten Hauptsatzes und die Konjunktion *and* entfallen.
- Die Verbform des zweiten Hauptsatzes wird durch das Partizip ersetzt.

He did his homework and he listened to the radio.
He did his homework listening to the radio.
Er machte seine Hausaufgaben und hörte Radio.

9 Passiv – *passive voice*

Bildung
Form von *to be* + Partizip Perfekt

Tower Bridge was finished in 1894.
Die Tower Bridge wurde 1894 fertig gestellt.

Zeitform

- *simple present*
  - Aktiv: Peter buys the milk.
  - Passiv: The milk is bought by Peter.

- *simple past*
  - Aktiv: Peter bought the milk.
  - Passiv: The milk was bought by Peter.

- *present perfect*
  - Aktiv: Peter has bought the milk.
  - Passiv: The milk has been bought by Peter.

- *past perfect*
  - Aktiv: Peter had bought the milk.
  - Passiv: The milk had been bought by Peter.

- *future I*
  - Aktiv: Peter will buy the milk.
  - Passiv: The milk will be bought by Peter.

- *future II*
  - Aktiv: Peter will have bought the milk.
  - Passiv: The milk will have been bought by Peter.

- *conditional I*
  - Aktiv: Peter would buy the milk.
  - Passiv: The milk would be bought by Peter.

- *conditional II*
  - Aktiv: Peter would have bought the milk.
  - Passiv: The milk would have been bought by Peter.

Aktiv → Passiv

Beachte bei der Umwandlung vom Aktiv ins Passiv:

- Das Subjekt des Aktivsatzes wird zum Objekt des Passivsatzes und mit *by* angeschlossen.
- Das Objekt des Aktivsatzes wird zum Subjekt des Passivsatzes.
- Stehen im Aktivsatz zwei Objekte (direktes und indirektes Objekt), lassen sich zwei verschiedene Passivsätze bilden. Eines der Objekte wird zum Subjekt des Passivsatzes, während das zweite Objekt bleibt.

Beachte:
Das indirekte Objekt muss im Passivsatz mit *to* angeschlossen werden.

Aktiv: <u>Peter</u> buys <u>the milk</u>.
      Subjekt   *Objekt*

Passiv: <u>The milk</u> is bought <u>by Peter</u>.
      Subjekt   *Objekt*

Aktiv: <u>They</u> gave <u>her</u> <u>a ball</u>.
      Subjekt   *ind. Obj.* *dir. Obj.*

Passiv: <u>She</u> was given <u>a ball</u>.
      Subjekt   *dir. Obj.*

oder:

Aktiv: <u>They</u> gave <u>her</u> <u>a ball</u>.
      Subjekt   *ind. Obj.* *dir. Obj.*

Passiv: <u>A ball</u> was given <u>to her</u>.
      Subjekt   *ind. Obj.*

Passiv → Aktiv

Beachte bei der Umwandlung vom Passiv ins Aktiv:

- Das mit *by* angeschlossene Objekt des Passivsatzes wird zum Subjekt des Aktivsatzes; *by* entfällt.
- Das Subjekt des Passivsatzes wird zum Objekt des Aktivsatzes.
- Wenn im Passivsatz der mit *by* angeschlossene Handelnde fehlt, muss im Aktivsatz ein Handelnder als Subjekt ergänzt werden, z. B. durch *somebody, we, you, they*.

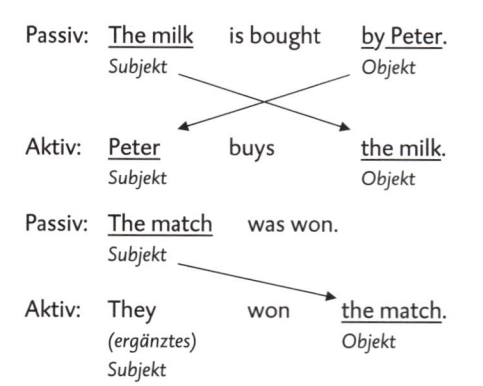

Passiv: <u>The milk</u> is bought <u>by Peter</u>.
      Subjekt   *Objekt*

Aktiv: <u>Peter</u> buys <u>the milk</u>.
      Subjekt   *Objekt*

Passiv: <u>The match</u> was won.
      Subjekt

Aktiv: They won <u>the match</u>.
     (ergänztes)   *Objekt*
     Subjekt

10 Präpositionen – *prepositions*

Präpositionen *(prepositions)* werden auch als Verhältniswörter bezeichnet. Sie drücken **räumliche, zeitliche oder andere Arten von Beziehungen** aus.

The ball is <u>under</u> the table.
Der Ball ist unter dem Tisch.

He came <u>after</u> six o'clock.
Er kam nach sechs Uhr.

I knew it <u>from</u> the start.
Ich wusste es von Anfang an.

Kurzgrammatik zum schnellen Nachschlagen und Auffinden

Die wichtigsten Präpositionen mit Beispielen für ihre Verwendung:

- *at*

  Ortsangabe: *at home*

  I'm <u>at home</u> at the moment.
  Ich bin zurzeit zu Hause.

  Zeitangabe: *at three o'clock*

  He arrived <u>at three o'clock</u>.
  Er kam um drei Uhr an.

- *by*

  Angabe des Mittels: *to go by bike*

  She went to work <u>by bike</u>.
  Sie fuhr mit dem Rad zur Arbeit.

  Angabe der Ursache: *by mistake*

  He did it <u>by mistake</u>.
  Er hat es aus Versehen getan.

  Zeitangabe: *by tomorrow*

  You will get your DVD back <u>by tomorrow</u>.
  Du bekommst deine DVD bis morgen zurück.

- *for*

  Zeitdauer: *for hours*

  We waited for the bus <u>for hours</u>.
  Wir haben stundenlang auf den Bus gewartet.

- *from*

  Ortsangabe: *from Dublin*

  Ian comes <u>from Dublin</u>.
  Ian kommt aus Dublin.

  Zeitangabe: *from nine to five*

  We work <u>from nine to five</u>.
  Wir arbeiten von neun bis fünf Uhr.

- *in*

  Ortsangabe: *in England*

  <u>In England</u>, they drive on the left.
  In England herrscht Linksverkehr.

  Zeitangabe: *in the morning*

  They woke up early <u>in the morning</u>.
  Sie wachten am frühen Morgen auf.

- *of*

  Ortsangabe: *north of the city*

  The village lies <u>north of the city</u>.
  Das Dorf liegt nördlich der Stadt.

- *on*

  Ortsangabe: *on the left, on the floor*

  <u>On the left</u> you see the Empire State Building.
  Links sehen Sie das Empire State Building.

  Zeitangabe: *on Monday*

  <u>On Monday</u> she will buy the tickets.
  (Am) Montag kauft sie die Karten.

- *to*

  Richtungsangabe: *to turn to the left*

  Please <u>turn to the left</u>.
  Bitte wenden Sie sich nach links.

  Angabe des Ziels: *to London*

  He goes <u>to London</u> every year.
  Er fährt jedes Jahr nach London.

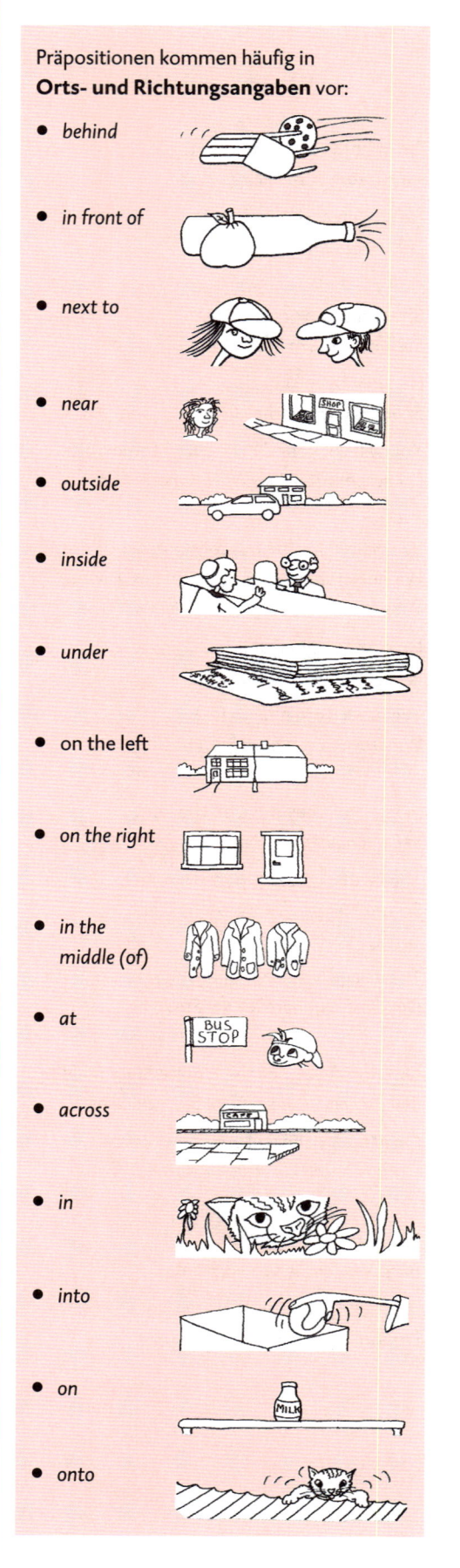

Präpositionen kommen häufig in **Orts- und Richtungsangaben** vor:

- behind — The ball is behind the chair.
- in front of — The apple is in front of the bottle.
- next to — Kim is next to Colin.
- near — Jenny is near the shop.
- outside — My car is outside my house.
- inside — Paula is inside the bank.
- under — The letter is under the book.
- on the left — My house is on the left.
- on the right — The door is on the right.
- in the middle (of) — My coat is in the middle. The bookshop is in the middle of the town.
- at — He is waiting at the bus stop.
- across — The café is across the street. She walks across the road.
- in — The cat is in the garden.
- into — Susan is putting the ball into the box.
- on — The milk is on the table.
- onto — The cat is climbing onto the garage roof.

- to

She drives <u>to</u> work.

- towards

Max is walking <u>towards</u> the cinema.

11 Relativsätze – *relative clauses*

Ein Relativsatz bezieht sich auf eine Person oder Sache des Hauptsatzes und beschreibt diese näher:

The boy <u>who looks like Jane</u> is her brother.
Der Junge, <u>der Jane ähnlich sieht</u>, ist ihr Bruder.

- Hauptsatz:

The boy is her brother

- Relativsatz:

who looks like Jane

Bildung
Haupt- und Nebensatz werden durch das Relativpronomen *(who, which, that)* verbunden.

- ***who*** bezieht sich auf **Personen**.

Peter, <u>who lives in London</u>, likes travelling.
Peter, <u>der in London lebt</u>, reist gerne.

- ***which*** bezieht sich auf **Sachen**.

The film "Dark Moon", <u>which we saw yesterday</u>, was far too long.
Der Film „Dark Moon", <u>den wir gestern sahen</u>, war viel zu lang.

- ***that*** bezieht sich auf **Sachen** und auf **Personen** und wird nur verwendet, wenn die **Information** im Relativsatz **notwendig** ist, um den ganzen Satz zu verstehen.

The film <u>that we saw last week</u> was much better.
Der Film, <u>den wir letzte Woche sahen</u>, war viel besser.

Verwendung
Mit Relativsätzen kannst du **aus zwei Sätzen einen Satz bilden**, wenn die beiden Sätze dasselbe Subjekt haben.

<u>London</u> is England's biggest city. <u>London</u> has about 7.2 million inhabitants.
London ist Englands größte Stadt. London hat etwa 7,2 Millionen Einwohner.

London, which is England's biggest city, has about 7.2 million inhabitants.
London, Englands größte Stadt, hat etwa 7,2 Millionen Einwohner.

12 Steigerung und Vergleich – *comparisons*

Steigerung des Adjektivs – *comparisons of adjectives*

Bildung

Man unterscheidet
- Grundform — Peter is y<u>oung</u>.
- 1. Steigerungsform — Jane is y<u>ounger</u>.
- 2. Steigerungsform — Paul is the y<u>oungest</u>.

Steigerung auf *-er, -est*
- einsilbige Adjektive

  old, old<u>er</u>, old<u>est</u>
  alt, älter, am ältesten

- zweisilbige Adjektive, die auf *-er, -le, -ow* oder *-y* enden

  clever, clever<u>er</u>, clever<u>est</u>
  klug, klüger, am klügsten

  simple, simpl<u>er</u>, simpl<u>est</u>
  einfach, einfacher, am einfachsten

  narrow, narrow<u>er</u>, narrow<u>est</u>
  eng, enger, am engsten

  funny, funn<u>ier</u>, funn<u>iest</u>
  lustig, lustiger, am lustigsten

Beachte:
- stummes *-e* am Wortende entfällt

  simpl<u>e</u>, simpl<u>er</u>, simpl<u>est</u>

- nach einem Konsonanten wird *-y* am Wortende zu *-i-*

  funn<u>y</u>, funn<u>ier</u>, funn<u>iest</u>

- nach kurzem Vokal wird ein Konsonant am Wortende verdoppelt

  fi<u>t</u>, fi<u>tt</u>er, fi<u>tt</u>est

Steigerung mit *more ..., most ...*
- zweisilbige Adjektive, die nicht auf *-er, -le, -ow* oder *-y* enden

  useful, <u>more</u> useful, <u>most</u> useful
  nützlich, nützlicher, am nützlichsten

- Adjektive mit drei und mehr Silben

  difficult, <u>more</u> difficult, <u>most</u> difficult
  schwierig, schwieriger, am schwierigsten

Unregelmäßige Steigerung

Die unregelmäßig gesteigerten Adjektive solltest du lernen. Einige wichtige Adjektive sind hier angegeben.

good, better, best
gut, besser, am besten

bad, worse, worst
schlecht, schlechter, am schlechtesten

many, more, most
viele, mehr, am meisten

much, more, most
viel, mehr, am meisten

little, less, least
wenig, weniger, am wenigsten

Vergleich – *sentences with comparisons*

Bildung

- Wenn du sagen möchtest, dass **zwei Sachen gleich** sind:
  as + Grundform des Adjektivs + *as*

  Anne is <u>as</u> tall <u>as</u> John.
  Anne ist genauso groß wie John.

- Wenn du sagen möchtest, dass **zwei Sachen ungleich** sind:
  not as + Grundform des Adjektivs + *as*

  John is <u>not as</u> tall <u>as</u> Steve.
  John ist nicht so groß wie Steve.

- Wenn du sagen möchtest, dass **zwei Sachen verschieden** gut/schlecht/schön … sind:
  1. Steigerungsform des Adjektivs + *than*

  Steve is <u>taller</u> <u>than</u> Anne.
  Steve ist größer als Anne.

Steigerung des Adverbs – *comparison of adverbs of manner*

Adverbien können wie Adjektive auch gesteigert werden.

- Adverbien auf *-ly* werden mit **more, most** bzw. mit **less, least** gesteigert.

  She talks <u>more</u> quickly than John.
  Sie spricht schneller als John.

- Adverbien, die dieselbe Form wie das Adjektiv haben, werden mit *-er, -est* gesteigert.

  fast – fast<u>er</u> – fast<u>est</u>
  early – earl<u>ier</u> – earl<u>iest</u>

- unregelmäßige Steigerungsformen haben:

  well – better – best
  badly – worse – worst

13 Wortstellung – *word order*

Im englischen Aussagesatz gilt die Wortstellung <u>Subjekt</u> – <u>Prädikat</u> – <u>Objekt</u> (*subject – verb – object*):

- Das <u>Subjekt</u> gibt an, wer oder was etwas tut.

  <u>The cat</u>
  Die Katze

- Das <u>Prädikat</u> gibt an, was getan wird.

  <u>catches</u>
  fängt

- Das <u>Objekt</u> gibt an, worauf/auf wen sich die Tätigkeit bezieht.

  <u>a mouse</u>.
  eine Maus.

Beachte:

- Orts- und Zeitangaben stehen meist am Satzende.

  We will buy a new car <u>tomorrow</u>.
  Morgen werden wir ein neues Auto kaufen.

  Peter lives <u>in New York</u>.
  Peter wohnt in New York.

- Ortsangaben stehen vor Zeitangaben.

  He moved <u>to New York</u> <u>in June</u>.
  Er ist im Juni nach New York gezogen.

14 Zeiten – *tenses*

Gegenwart – *simple present*

Bildung

Grundform des Verbs, Ausnahme 3. Person Singular: Grundform des Verbs + -s

stand – he/she/it stand<u>s</u>

Beachte:
- Bei Verben, die auf -s, -sh, -ch, -x enden, wird -es angefügt.

kis<u>s</u> – he/she/it kiss<u>es</u>
ru<u>sh</u> – he/she/it rush<u>es</u>
tea<u>ch</u> – he/she/it teach<u>es</u>
fi<u>x</u> – he/she/it fix<u>es</u>

- Bei Verben, die auf Konsonant + -y enden, wird -es angefügt; -y wird zu -i-.

car<u>ry</u> – he/she/it carr<u>ies</u>

Bildung von Fragen im *simple present*

Umschreibung mit Fragewort + *do/does* + Grundform des Verbs

Where does he live?
Wo lebt er?

Beachte:
Die Umschreibung wird nicht verwendet,
- wenn nach dem Subjekt gefragt wird (mit *who, what, which*).

<u>Who</u> came to the party?
Wer kam zur Party?

<u>What</u> happens next?
Was passiert als Nächstes?

<u>Which</u> tree <u>has</u> more leaves?
Welcher Baum hat mehr Blätter?

- wenn die Frage mit *is/are* gebildet wird.

<u>Are</u> you happy?
Bist du glücklich?

Bildung der Verneinung im *simple present*

Umschreibung mit *don't/doesn't* + Grundform des Verbs

He <u>doesn't like</u> football.
Er mag Fußball nicht.

Verwendung

Das *simple present* beschreibt
- Tätigkeiten, die man gewohnheitsmäßig oder häufig ausführt,

Every morning John <u>buys</u> a newspaper.
Jeden Morgen kauft sich John eine Zeitung.

- allgemein gültige Aussagen.

London <u>is</u> a big city.
London ist eine große Stadt.

Signalwörter: *always, every morning, every afternoon, every day, often, never*

Kurzgrammatik zum schnellen Nachschlagen und Auffinden

Verlaufsform der Gegenwart – *present progressive*

Bildung
am/is/are + Verb in der *-ing*-Form (Partizip Präsens)

read → am/is/are reading

Bildung von Fragen im *present progressive*
am/is/are + Subjekt + Verb in der *-ing*-Form

Is Peter reading?
Liest Peter gerade?

Bildung der Verneinung im *present progressive*
am not/isn't/aren't + Verb in der *-ing*-Form

Peter isn't reading.
Peter liest gerade nicht.

Verwendung
Mit dem *present progressive* drückt man aus,
- dass etwas **gerade passiert** und **noch nicht abgeschlossen** ist.
  Signalwörter: *at the moment, now*

  At the moment, Peter is drinking a cup of tea.
  Im Augenblick trinkt Peter eine Tasse Tee.
  [Er hat damit angefangen und noch nicht aufgehört.]

- dass es um eine **zukünftige, bereits festgelegte Handlung** geht.

  We are watching the match on Sunday.
  Am Sonntag sehen wir uns das Spiel an.

simple past – 1. Vergangenheit

Bildung
Regelmäßige Verben: Grundform des Verbs + *-ed*

walk → walked

Beachte:
- stummes *-e* entfällt

  hope → hoped

- bei Verben, die auf Konsonant + *-y* enden, wird *-y* zu *-i-*

  carry → carried

- nach kurzem betonten Vokal wird der Schlusskonsonant verdoppelt

  stop → stopped

Unregelmäßige Verben: siehe die Liste in deinem Schulbuch. Die *simple-past*-Formen einiger wichtiger unregelmäßiger Verben sind hier angegeben.

be → was
have → had
give → gave
go → went
meet → met
say → said
see → saw
take → took
write → wrote

Bildung von Fragen im *simple past*
Umschreibung mit Fragewort + *did* + Grundform des Verbs

Why did he look out of the window?
Warum sah er aus dem Fenster?

Beachte:
Die Umschreibung wird nicht verwendet,
- wenn nach dem Subjekt gefragt wird (mit *who, what, which*).

    Who paid the bill?
    Wer zahlte die Rechnung?

    What happened to your friend?
    Was ist mit deinem Freund passiert?

    Which boy cooked the meal?
    Welcher Junge hat das Essen gekocht?

- wenn die Frage mit *were* gebildet wird.

    Were you happy?
    Warst du glücklich?

Bildung der Verneinung im *simple past*
Umschreibung mit *didn't* + Grundform des Verbs

Why didn't you call me?
Warum hast du mich nicht angerufen?

Verwendung
Das *simple past* beschreibt Handlungen und Ereignisse, die **in der Vergangenheit geschehen** und **bereits abgeschlossen** sind.
Signalwörter: *yesterday, last week, last year, (five years) ago, in (1999)*

Last week he helped me with my homework.
Letzte Woche half er mir bei meinen Hausaufgaben. [Die Hilfe fand in der letzten Woche statt, ist also bereits abgeschlossen.]

Verlaufsform der 1. Vergangenheit – *past progressive*

Bildung
was/were + Verb in der *-ing*-Form

watch → was/were watching

Verwendung
Das *past progressive* verwendet man, wenn zu einem bestimmten Zeitpunkt in der Vergangenheit eine Handlung abläuft.

Yesterday at 11 o'clock I was still sleeping.
Gestern um 11 Uhr habe ich noch geschlafen.

I was reading a book when Peter came into the room.
Ich las (gerade) ein Buch, als Peter ins Zimmer kam.

2. Vergangenheit – *present perfect simple*

Bildung
have/has + Partizip Perfekt des Verbs

write → has/have written

Verwendung

Das *present perfect simple* verwendet man, wenn

- ein Vorgang in der Vergangenheit begonnen hat und noch andauert,

  He has lived in London since 2002.
  Er lebt seit 2002 in London.
  [*Er lebt jetzt immer noch in London.*]

- das Ergebnis einer vergangenen Handlung **Auswirkungen auf die Gegenwart** hat.

  I have finished my work.
  Ich bin mit meiner Arbeit fertig.

Beachte:
have/has können zu *'ve/'s* verkürzt werden.

I've eaten your lunch.
Ich habe dein Mittagessen gegessen.

He's given me his umbrella.
Er hat mir seinen Regenschirm gegeben.

Signalwörter: *already, ever, just, how long, not ... yet, since, for*

Beachte:
Das *present perfect simple* wird oft mit *since* und *for* verwendet (deutsch: „seit").

- *since* gibt einen **Zeitpunkt** an.

  Ron has lived in Sydney since 1997.
  Ron lebt seit 1997 in Sydney.

- *for* gibt einen **Zeitraum** an.

  Sally has lived in Los Angeles for five years.
  Sally lebt seit fünf Jahren in Los Angeles.

Verlaufsform der 2. Vergangenheit – *present perfect progressive*

Bildung
have/has + *been* + Partizip Präsens

write → has/have been writing

Verwendung
Das *present perfect progressive* verwendet man, um die **Dauer einer Handlung** zu **betonen**, die in der Vergangenheit begonnen hat und noch andauert.

She has been sleeping for ten hours.
Sie schläft seit zehn Stunden.

Vorvergangenheit – *past perfect*

Bildung
had + Partizip Perfekt

write → had written

Verwendung

Das *past perfect* verwendet man, wenn ein Vorgang, der in der Vergangenheit abgeschlossen wurde, vor einem anderen Vorgang in der Vergangenheit stattfindet.

He had bought a ticket
Er hatte ein Ticket gekauft,

before he took the train to Manchester.
bevor er den Zug nach Manchester nahm.
[Beim Einsteigen war der Kauf abgeschlossen.]

Verlaufsform der Vorvergangenheit – *past perfect progressive*

Bildung
had + *been* + Partizip Präsens

write → had been writing

Verwendung

Das *past perfect progressive* verwendet man für Handlungen, die in der Vergangenheit bis zu dem Zeitpunkt andauern, zu dem eine neue Handlung einsetzt.

She had been sleeping for ten hours when the doorbell rang.
Sie hatte seit zehn Stunden geschlafen, als es an der Tür klingelte. [Das Schlafen dauerte bis zu dem Zeitpunkt an, als es an der Tür klingelte.]

Zukunft mit *will* – *will-future*

Bildung
will + Grundform des Verbs

buy → will buy

Bildung von Fragen im *will-future*
Fragewort + *will* + Grundform des Verbs

What will you buy? *Was wirst du kaufen?*

Bildung der Verneinung im *will-future*
Fragewort + *won't* + Grundform des Verbs

Why won't you come to our party?
Warum kommst du nicht zu unserer Party?

Verwendung

Das *will-future* verwendet man, wenn ein Vorgang **in der Zukunft stattfinden** wird. Signalwörter: *tomorrow, next week, next Monday, next year, in three years, soon*

The holidays will start next week.
Nächste Woche beginnen die Ferien.

Beachte: Bei geplanten Handlungen verwendet man das *going-to-future*.

Zukunft mit *going to* – *going-to-future*

Bildung
am/is/are + *going to* + Grundform des Verbs

find → am/is/are going to find

Verwendung

Das *going-to-future* verwendet man, um auszudrücken, dass eine **Handlung geplant** ist.

I am going to work in England this summer.
Diesen Sommer werde ich in England arbeiten.

Notizen

Notizen

▶ **Original-Aufgaben der Abschlussprüfung an Realschulen in Hamburg**

Schriftliche Realschulprüfung Hamburg
Englisch 2005

Job interviews

Mike has never forgotten his first job interview. He was well prepared and confident he could answer any questions the interviewer might ask him. Unfortunately, however, it all went horribly wrong: "I knocked firmly on the door, walked in, smiled and sat down," he remembers. "The interview was going brilliantly until I looked down and noticed blood dripping from my hand. I must have cut it on the nameplate on the door when I knocked. I froze: Had the interviewer seen? Had I got blood on him? Did I need a doctor? I got out a tissue[1] and tried to mop up the blood, while continuing to answer his questions. He behaved[2] as if he had not noticed, but I could tell he wasn't impressed. I didn't get the job, of course."

Accidents will happen – but Mike's experience shows an important point: no matter how qualified, experienced and well prepared you are, you won't impress an interviewer if your body lets you down[3]. You may be able to speak like a politician and your vocabulary might be as good as Shakespeare's, but the story that your body language tells is as important as anything that comes out of your mouth.

So how can you make sure you do well in an interview? You could hire an actor to stand in for you at your interview or you could just teach your body to behave itself. It's not as hard as it sounds. All you need is a mirror, a video-camera and a cat. Most people have no idea how other people see them. They can't tell if their words are backed up[4] by the tone of their voice and posture[5]. When you prepare for an interview it's important not just to practise what you have to say, but **how** you say it. The best way to see how you appear to others is to practise in front of a mirror. If you can, you should videotape yourself and ask friends for feedback. If there's nobody around, practise with your cat. The more prepared you are, the more relaxed and confident you'll feel – and appear.

When it comes to the interview itself sit up comfortably and lean slightly forward so you look attentive[6]. Breathe slowly. And make sure your clothes aren't too tight: it won't give a good impression if you lift your arm and your jacket buttons fly off. And yes, it is a good idea to visit the toilet before your interview, particularly if you're nervous. There is no point trying to lie in an interview. Just be yourself. If you say what you mean and mean what you say your verbal and non-verbal communication will match. Any interviewer is interested in who you really are.

Text adapted from: "BodyLanguage" by Hilary Freeman, in The Guardian, April 6, 2004

1 tissue – Papier(taschen)tuch
2 behave – sich (gut) benehmen
3 let somebody down – jemanden im Stich lassen
4 back up – unterstützen, stärken
5 posture – (Körper)haltung
6 attentive – aufmerksam

1.1 Leseverstehen: *Right – wrong – not in the text*

Read the text 'Job interviews' and the sentences on your worksheet carefully. Is the information *right* or *wrong* or *not in the text*? Tick (✓) right box.

		right	wrong	not in text
1.	Mike probably injured his hand when he knocked on the door.	☐	☐	☐
2.	He did not know if he needed a doctor.	☐	☐	☐
3.	Mike was so shocked to see the blood on his hand he could no longer answer the interviewer's questions.	☐	☐	☐
4.	The interviewer offered Mike a tissue.	☐	☐	☐
5.	Mike's first job interview was not a success.	☐	☐	☐
6.	Body language is far more important than what you actually say in an interview.	☐	☐	☐
7.	Most people try to impress the interviewer with very clever answers.	☐	☐	☐
8.	Politicians sometimes use the language of Shakespeare.	☐	☐	☐
9.	You can teach your body to behave itself.	☐	☐	☐
10.	Most people know how others see them.	☐	☐	☐
11.	You should practise how to say things in an interview.	☐	☐	☐
12.	Friends can be helpful when you prepare for an interview.	☐	☐	☐
13.	First practise with your cat and then ask friends for feedback!	☐	☐	☐
14.	Good preparation makes you feel more confident in interviews.	☐	☐	☐
15.	Always give the interviewer a nice smile when you walk into the room!	☐	☐	☐
16.	Mike bought a blue jacket for the interview.	☐	☐	☐
17.	Lean back comfortably during the interview!	☐	☐	☐
18.	Visit the toilet before the interview!	☐	☐	☐
19.	Be yourself in job interviews!	☐	☐	☐
20.	Mike wrote a book about job interviews.	☐	☐	☐

1.2 Leseverstehen: *Matching*

Job ads

Imagine you are looking for a job and you have clear ideas of what you would like to do. Which job would you apply for?

Step 1: Look at the sentences on the worksheet (page 4).
Step 2: Read through the job ads carefully.
Step 3: Tick (✓) <u>all</u> ads that advertise jobs which fit the information given on the left.
In some cases there might be more than one possibility.

Jeder richtig gesetzte Haken = 1 Punkt.
Setze Haken nur, wenn du dir sicher bist.
Jeder falsch gesetzte Haken innerhalb einer Teilaufgabe führt zum Abzug von 0,5 Punkten.

A
OFFICE ASSISTANT REQUIRED
Flexible 12–15 hours per week in our busy St Albans Design/Build office, helping with all aspects of office administration. Must be confident in Microsoft Office and have good telephone manner.
Further details from Civic Construction 01727 868516

B
MARKET RESEARCH INTERVIEWERS
- Earn £ 55.00 – £ 60.10 for a 6 hour working day.
- **Other benefits:** travel allowance and holiday pay.
- **Flexible work:** min. 2 and up to 5 days per week.
- **No previous experience:** full training given.
- **No selling:** asking people's opinions in their homes.

If you enjoy working on your own, can work after 1.30pm or at weekends, have **your own transport** and **land phone line**, and want to find out more, phone us now for an information pack quoting your postcode and code no: **3823JW**

01482 401272

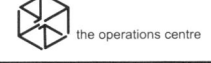

BMRB INTERNATIONAL the operations centre

C
FORDS
of Newton Bridge
have vacancies for
RESTAURANT ASSISTANTS

In their busy Oak Room Restaurant, applicants should be able to work under pressure, normal working hours, 8.30am – 5.50pm, 5 days a week.

Company offers competitive salary, 4 weeks annual holiday and generous staff discounts.

Please call at our First Floor Reception Desk for an application form or write with your details to

Personnel
FORDS DEPARTMENT STORE
16 Palace St. Newton Bridge
ZQ12 2OU

D
NOAH'S ARK IS EXPANDING
We require a
TEAM LEADER
with 3 years post qualifying experience

Also
NURSERY NURSES

Call Denny on
01438 749090

E
Commercial Estate Agents require
SECRETARY/ PERSONAL ASSISTANT

To carry out a wide variety of duties in busy office.
Must be confident dealing with the public.
Word processing knowledge essential.
Salary by negotiation

Reply in writing, enclosing CV to:
WORTHING COMMERCIAL

**36 FLEET STREET
EXETER EX1 9BB**

Example:

	A	B	C	D	E
You would like to work as a restaurant assistant.			✓		

Now it is your turn:

	A	B	C	D	E
You would like to work three days per week, you have your own car and you enjoy talking to people.					
You want at least three weeks of holiday per year.					
You are used to all sorts of office work.					
You would like to work at an estate agent's.					
You have always enjoyed working with young children and would like to work in a nursery.					
You do not want to work more than 14 hours per week.					
You can work well under pressure.					
You would like to work close to your home in Exeter.					

2 Textproduktion: *Writing a letter*

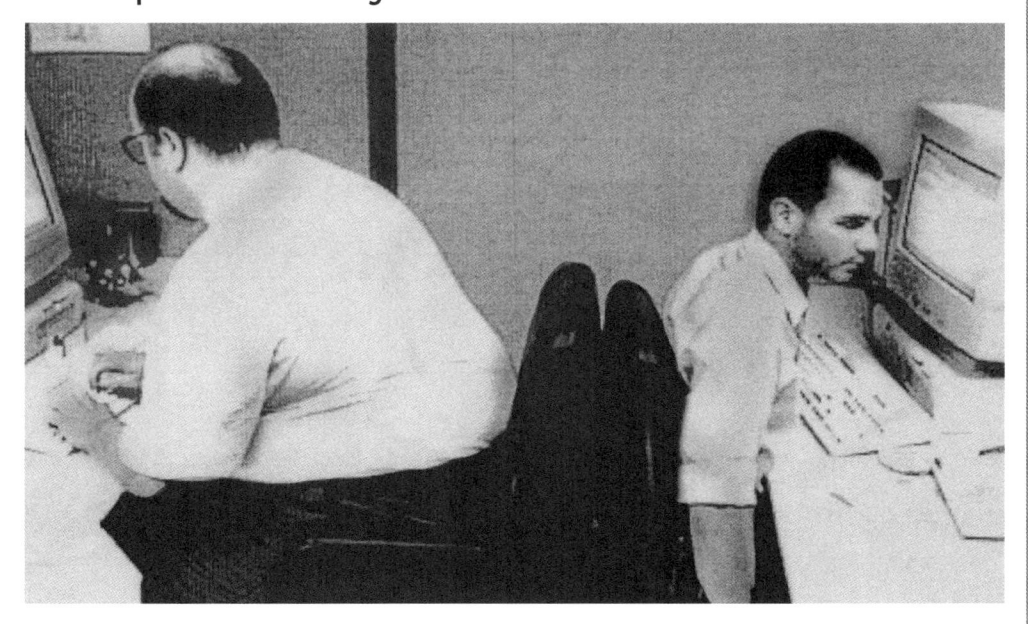

Imagine you are one of the two employees in the picture and you are not satisfied with the working conditions in your office.
Write a letter to your boss whom you do not know very well.
- **Describe** the working conditions (**place, colleagues, type of work, atmosphere**) in the office shown in the picture
- and **complain** about them.
- **Ask** your boss to do something about the problem.

Sender: Fred Flint, 46, High Street, Exeter EX 1 9BB
Addressee: Mr John Dunn, 102, Fleet Street, Exeter EX1 9BB

You should write at least 150 words. Do not write more than 200 words.

Please count your words before you hand in your paper. But do not include the words of the date and the addresses of the sender and addressee.
A short form (e.g. I'm, he's, isn't) counts as one word.

number of words:

3 Sprechen (English in use): Applying for a job

Du telefonierst mit dem Personalchef eines Kaufhauses in London und informierst dich über die Möglichkeit, dort einen Arbeitsplatz zu bekommen. Du erzählst in englischer Sprache über dich, denn dein Gesprächspartner spricht kein Deutsch.

Bei dieser Aufgabe geht es **nicht um die wörtliche Übersetzung**, sondern um die passende Wiedergabe auf Englisch in maximal zwei Sätzen.

Manchmal gibt es mehrere Möglichkeiten, die Aussage zu formulieren. Entscheide dich für eine Möglichkeit. Wenn du eine Vokabel nicht kennst, dann versuche sie auf Englisch zu umschreiben.

1. Du nennst deinen Namen **und** sagst, dass du dich gern um eine Stelle als Verkäufer/in bewerben würdest. — 3 Punkte

2. Du berichtest, dass du die Stellenanzeigen gestern in der Zeitung gelesen hast **und** dass du sehr interessiert warst.

3. Du erklärst, dass du bei einer englischen Firma arbeiten möchtest, **weil** du schon immer in England leben und arbeiten wolltest. — 3 Punkte

4. Du nennst dein Alter **und** sagst, dass du bereits in vielen Kaufhäusern in Deutschland gearbeitet hast. — 3 Punkte

5. Du sagst, dass du gerne mit Menschen arbeitest **und** dass du auch Freude daran hast, anderen zu helfen. — 3 Punkte

6. Am Ende sagst du deutlich, dass du dich über die Möglichkeit eines Vorstellungsgespräches sehr freuen würdest **und** auf eine baldige Antwort hoffst. — 3 Punkte

3.1 Sprachliche Mittel

Choose the correct word

Read the following text carefully. Choose and tick (✓) the correct words in the grid. Words followed by a * are explained below the text.

Hotel Boat Staff

This is an interesting job where you can show your catering and hospitality* skills. You can also _____ (1) the great outdoors as you travel around the country. Hotel Boats drive through the canals and rivers in England and Wales, and offer 7 nights _____ (2). Because of working with the owners and having only 9 passengers per week you _____ (3) in a small friendly family environment, ideal for people who like to travel and work alone. If you are an all-rounder who hates to be indoors we have your dream job.

We want to employ three young people to work with our Hotel Boat crew that works on the canals & rivers in England & Wales. _____ (4) will start immediately until the middle of October which is the end _____ (5) our boating season. You will work with the owners Steve & Steph. You _____ (6) also help with cleaning and working the boat.

There are also two free positions on our Hotel Boats Snipe and Taurus where you work with the owners Derek & Emma. Here, it would be an advantage if you _____ (7) good at cooking but it's not important because you will assist Emma. You also assist with boating and cleaning.

Important _____ (8) for all the jobs are that you are physically fit and used to an outdoor life. If you are fit, active and enthusiastic we should be able to train you to do all the tasks which have to do with boating. However, if you don't even know _____ (9) to make a cake or lay a table properly we will not accept you because the domestic work* is _____ (10) important to us.

hospitality = Gastfreundschaft
domestic work = Hausarbeit

Choose and tick the correct words in the grid below:

1	make	have fun	need	enjoy
2	holiday's	holidays'	holidays	holidais
3	will be	are being	were	had been
4	Employed	Employer	Employable	Employment
5	from	with	of	by
6	must	needn't	mustn't	haven't
7	could	were	be	can
8	qualities	quality	qualifies	qualifying
9	that	how	who	which
10	many	some	a lot of	most

3.2 Synonyms

Find synonyms which can replace the underlined words in the text. Fill only **one** synonym for each of the underlined words into the grid. A synonym may consist of more than one word.

8 Punkte

Resort Work

Resorts offer many summer jobs and some winter jobs, especially for students who are looking for seasonal work. The most common jobs in resorts are waiter or waitress, dishwasher, chambermaid or other hotel work. Your duties may not be very exciting, but you can often work in a beautiful (1) and peaceful work environment where you can become friends with many (2) Americans. There are resorts throughout the U.S. See our web site to find lists of them.

Hotel Work

Hotel work is similar to resort work, and the jobs are often low-level. Most are for chambermaids, but there are also positions at the front desk, in the hotel laundry, in restaurant facilities, hotel maintenance, etc. The salaries (3) for most of the jobs are lower because you can improve your salaries by earning tips.

Restaurant Work

Restaurant work is easy to find. It might be tiring (4) to do, but you come into contact with different types of people, and can make good money through tips. Most restaurant jobs are found by walking in and speaking (5) to the restaurant manager.

Department Stores

The American department store offers a variety of employment opportunities (6). The most common job is sales assistant, helping customers or working the cash registers. Large department stores are open six or seven days a week, and many are open in the evenings. This will enable you to arrange a fairly flexible working schedule. Many stores hire (7) extra workers during the busy Christmas shopping season, which begins (8) around Thanksgiving (late November). Supermarkets have high staff demands for workers. Most openings are for cashiers, stock clerk, and sales assistant. The best way to find these jobs is to walk in with your résumé* and ask to see the manager.

Text adapted from: CIEE

résumé (US) = Lebenslauf

Synonyms:

1	beautiful	
2	many	
3	salaries	
4	tiring	
5	speaking	
6	opportunities	
7	hire	
8	begins	

Schriftliche Realschulprüfung Hamburg
Englisch 2006

2006-1

1.1 Hörverstehen: *Tick the pictures*

Safe outback travel
- You have **three minutes** to read the following introduction and to look at the pictures before you listen to the CD.
- Now listen to this safe outback travel advice from the Royal Flying Doctor Service. You will hear it twice.
- Tick those pictures which show people and things mentioned in the travel advice.

Introduction
We talked to Chief Medical Officer, Dr Bruce Sanderson from the South Eastern Section of Royal Flying Doctor Service.

8 Punkte

a) ☐   b) ☐   c) ☐   d) ☐

e) ☐   f) ☐   g) ☐   h) ☐

i) ☐   j) ☐   k) ☐   l) ☐

1.2 Hörverstehen: *Right/wrong/no information*

Coral wonders

12 Punkte

- You have **five minutes** to read the following introduction and statements before listening to the speaker.
- You will hear the text twice.
- Tick the right box. The statement is either right (✓) wrong (✓) or there is no information (✓) about it.

Introduction

The Great Barrier Reef in north-eastern Australia is one of the world's natural wonders. It is also the world's largest living organism – you can even see it from the moon! On land, the best place to find out more about this wonder is Reef HQ in Townsville, Queensland. Reef HQ is an aquarium and the home of the world's largest living indoor coral reef. Tawnee Birtles, 18, tells you what it is like to work there.

		right	wrong	no information
1.	Tawnee doesn't like speaking to people from other countries.	☐	☐	☐
2.	She is a Reef HQ volunteer.	☐	☐	☐
3.	Tawnee lives in Townsville, Queensland.	☐	☐	☐
4.	She always wanted to become a volunteer at Reef HQ.	☐	☐	☐
5.	First she learned about the reef fish and plants.	☐	☐	☐
6.	As soon as she started training they let her work with the coral.	☐	☐	☐
7.	At the Reef HQ they make new coral colonies which you can visit in the aquarium.	☐	☐	☐
8.	A piece of coral is a whole colony of polyps.	☐	☐	☐
9.	Tawnee is an assistant tour guide at Reef HQ.	☐	☐	☐
10.	She likes her job a lot.	☐	☐	☐
11.	She doesn't like talking German to the tourists from Germany and Switzerland, though.	☐	☐	☐
12.	One day she was attacked by a shark.	☐	☐	☐

1.3 Leseverstehen: *Multiple choice*

Step 1: Read the newspaper article "Shark attack – Surfer fights off" and the sentences on your worksheet carefully.

Shark attack – Surfer fights off

Thursday, 8 September 2005

Shark attack survivor Jake Heron credits his surfboard with saving his life when a great white shark attacked him at Fishery Bay, south of Port Lincoln on Sunday. The 30-year-old fisherman is in no hurry to get back in the water and it is unlikely he would return to surf in the same area.

Mr Heron said he had surfed at Fishery Bay for years and never seen a shark. He told of punching and kicking the four-metre long shark to survive. "I just looked around and saw a black tail and then I felt the bite, so I knew I'd been bitten." Mr Heron said everything happened very quickly and he doesn't remember feeling any pain at the time. After the initial attack he said the shark latched onto his surfboard and dragged it under the water, ending up about three metres away from him.

His friend, Craig Matena was surfing with him at the time and said his friend's cries for help alerted him to trouble. "I could hear Jake. The cries for help stick in my mind," Mr Matena said. "A shark attack was the first thing that came to my mind." Mr Heron said he didn't see the shark before it attacked but he believes it was a great white. "I know what a bronze whaler looks like, I'm an experienced fisherman, and it definitely wasn't one of them." According to Mr Heron's opinion the Department of Fisheries should start controlling the number of sharks in Port Lincoln.

Some people think that the tuna industry in this area is the reason for the increasing number of white sharks whereas others say that there have always been sharks in this area, even before the tuna industry was established.

Mr Zacharin, the director of the Department of Fisheries, has rejected claims that the tuna industry had increased the likelihood of attacks. Tuna industry spokesperson Brian Jeffriess said great whites had been in the area at this time of year for many years before the tuna industry was established.

Mr Heron said he believed the number of sharks was increasing and this time of year when tuna harvesting coming to an end was particularly dangerous. "I wouldn't be going surfing at left point (where the attack happened) today and for September just be pretty wary. The authorities have just got to get the number of sharks down because they've got no natural enemies." Mr Zacharin said great white sharks were protected under State and Federal law and it was fisheries' role to carry out current policy. Friend of Mr Heron and fellow surfer in the water at the time of the attack Craig Matena said water sports were a big part of his life growing up in Port Lincoln but things had changed. "There's no way I'd go out in that bay now. The authorities really need to take a good look at it. Something needs to be done about it – not just talk about it."

Text based on a report by Billie Harrison, Port Lincoln Times

Step 2:

Tick (✓) the correct answer. Only one answer (A, B or C) is correct.

1. Jake Heron is
   - A ☐ an old fisherman
   - B ☐ an Australian surf champion
   - C ☐ an amateur surfer

2. Heron was attacked by a shark
   - A ☐ near Port Lincoln
   - B ☐ south of Fishery Bay
   - C ☐ while in his boat

3. Mr Heron will
   - A ☐ go back to surfing immediately
   - B ☐ go back to surfing within the next few days
   - C ☐ probably not go back to surfing in the same area

4. The tuna industry
   - A ☐ is the reason for the increasing number of sharks in the area
   - B ☐ is believed to be the reason for the increasing number of sharks in the area
   - C ☐ should start controlling the number of sharks in the area

5. Port Lincoln authorities
   - A ☐ have already reduced the number of sharks
   - B ☐ should reduce the number of sharks
   - C ☐ are the sharks' natural enemies

6. Sharks are
   - A ☐ protected by Mr Zacharin
   - B ☐ without natural enemies
   - C ☐ important for the tuna industry

7. Brian Jeffriess is
   - A ☐ employed by the tuna industry
   - B ☐ an expert on sharks
   - C ☐ to blame for the shark problem

20 Punkte

8. "for September just be pretty wary" means that
   A ☐ surfers should be careful in September
   B ☐ surfers should refrain from surfing
   C ☐ surfing in September is recommended by State and Federal law

9. Craig Matena
   A ☐ did not notice that this friend had been attacked
   B ☐ saw the shark that attacked his friend
   C ☐ heard his friend's cries for help

10. Mr Matena wants the authorities
    A ☐ to take action
    B ☐ to talk about the problem
    C ☐ to arrange a meeting

2 Textproduktion: *Writing an email*

You are on an exchange visit to Australia. You have just come back from a trip with your host family. Since you know that your class is waiting for some news you send an email to your English teacher telling him/her about your trip.
- write about what you visited and when, referring to four of the seven pictures below,
- write about what you did there,
- tell your teacher what the highlight of your trip was and say why,
- give some information about the climate,
- say what you didn't like,
- think up an email address for your teacher and yourself and write the subject of your mail.

Write between 150–200 words. Don't forget to write full sentences.

Aborigines

Twelve Apostles
situated at the Great Ocean Road, Victoria

Sydney Harbour Bridge

Uluru

Kookaburra

Dingo

Datei Bearbeiten Ansicht Einfügen Format Extras Aktionen ?
Senden
Optionen...
Arial
10
F K U
An...
Cc...
Betreff:

3 Sprechen (English in use): At the tourist information office

Bei dieser Aufgabe geht es **nicht um die wörtliche Übersetzung**, sondern um die passende Wiedergabe auf Englisch in maximal zwei Sätzen.
Manchmal gibt es mehrere Möglichkeiten, die Aussage zu formulieren. Entscheide dich für eine Möglichkeit.

Du bist in Sydney auf dem Flughafen angekommen, hast noch keine Unterkunft und erkundigst dich bei der „tourist information" nach verschiedenen Möglichkeiten. Du musst natürlich auf Englisch fragen.

3 Punkte 1. Du sagst, dass du gerade in Sydney angekommen bist **und** eine preiswerte Unterkunft im Zentrum suchst.

3 Punkte 2. Du fragst höflich nach einem Stadtplan **und** bittest darum, dir zu zeigen, wo sich die nächstgelegene Jugendherberge befindet.

3 Punkte 3. Du sagst, dass du nichts über das Verkehrssystem in Sydney weißt **und** fragst, wie du am besten zur Jugendherberge kommst.

3 Punkte 4. Du fragst auch nach Informationen zu Sehenswürdigkeiten in Sydney **und** fragst, ob es Schülerermäßigung gibt.

3 Punkte 5. Du erklärst, dass du den Stadtführer gut findest, er dir aber zu teuer ist **und** du lieber einige kostenlose Prospekte mitnehmen möchtest.

3 Punkte 6. Du bedankst dich für die Hilfe, wünscht deinem Gegenüber einen schönen Tag **und** verabschiedest dich.

3.1 Sprachliche Mittel: *Choose the correct word*

Read the text below and decide which answer A, B, C or D best fits each space. **Tick (✓) the correct word!** There is an example at the beginning (0).

10 Punkte

Example:

| 0. | A | | live | B | | life | C | ✓ | living | D | | lived |

My Story

I earn my _____ (0) on a sheep and cattle station 110 kilometres from the nearest town, Broken Hill although it hasn't been much of a living since the drought. On Valentines Day 2004, my daughter, my dad and I woke up early to muster the sheep for shearing. It was almost 6am and the sun _____ (1) when we started work. It was still pretty dark as I rode my motorbike, so I didn't see the large branch _____ (2) the road. The branch knocked my foot _____ (3) the pedal and impaled itself in my right foot, destroying one of my brand new boots! The branch must have snapped off a Mulga tree during the dry thunderstorm the night _____ (4). The Mulga tree _____ (5) in the Bush for being very poisonous. A scratch from a branch can give you the _____ (6) infection. My dad and daughter went back for the car, as I _____ (7) on the ground in agonising pain. They _____ (8) to the house and called the Flying Doctors. The nearest airstrip was _____ (9) wet for the aircraft to land so we drove to another strip, 17 miles away. Flight Nurse, Katie Taylor and Capt Magnus Badger _____ (10) when we arrived. They flew me to Broken Hill Base Hospital where I had three operations and plastic surgery over six weeks.

based on a report by Peter Herring, "Gum Park Station" via "Broken Hill" NSW Newsletter No 2/2004 (RFDS)

1.	A	☐	was rising	B	☐	rose	C	☐	was risen	D	☐	rises
2.	A	☐	nearest	B	☐	beside	C	☐	next	D	☐	at
3.	A	☐	on	B	☐	of	C	☐	off	D	☐	to
4.	A	☐	after	B	☐	later	C	☐	in front of	D	☐	before
5.	A	☐	is well known	B	☐	knows well	C	☐	is well knowing	D	☐	knows
6.	A	☐	worst	B	☐	worse	C	☐	baddest	D	☐	bad
7.	A	☐	laid	B	☐	lie	C	☐	lay	D	☐	lain
8.	A	☐	would drive me home	B	☐	rode me	C	☐	drive me back	D	☐	drove me back
9.	A	☐	to	B	☐	also	C	☐	too	D	☐	hardly
10.	A	☐	were here	B	☐	was there	C	☐	were there	D	☐	are there

3.2 Sprachliche Mittel: *Synonyms*

8 Punkte

Find synonyms for the underlined words and fill in the grid below.
Make sure you use the right form of the word, the right tense etc.

Example:

0	gifts	presents

ACTION FILE

0830 hours Christmas morning and I'm watching my three kids open their gifts (0) when the phone rings. The Sydney Medical Retrieval Unit requests (1) us to fly to Walgett to attend a woman in labour.

0930 hours Capt James Young and I dressed in Christmas hats and shirts, depart (2) for Walgett.

1010 hours On arrival we discover (3) the woman has already given birth to a baby boy. After giving mum and baby thorough examination, I give them the all clear.
James and I get ready to leave when we are advised (4) about a woman and her family, driving in to Walgett from Collarenebri who has serious (5) abdominal pain.

1030 hours James and I transfer (6) the patient to the aircraft (7). After a tearful goodbye for mum and kids, and with mum now with the Christmas Barbie doll to look after her, we take off for Dubbo.

1230 hours On arrival in Dubbo, the ambulance is at the hangar ready to transfer the patient to hospital where she has surgery later that day. The patient was discharged (8) two days later.

based on a report by Dubbo Base Senior Flight Nurse, Sharon Murphy

Synonyms:

1	requests	
2	depart	
3	discover	
4	are advised	
5	serious	
6	transfer	
7	aircraft	
8	was discharged	

Notizen

Ideal zum selbstständigen Lernen

Schülergerecht aufbereiteter Lernstoff mit anschaulichen Beispielen, abwechslungsreichen Übungen und erklärenden Lösungen zum selbstständigen Lernen zu Hause. Schließt Wissenslücken und gibt Sicherheit und Motivation durch Erfolgserlebnisse.

Mathematik

Mathematik Grundwissen 5. Klasse
Realschule Bayern .... Best.-Nr. 91410
Mathematik Grundwissen 6. Klasse
Realschule Bayern .... Best.-Nr. 914056
Mathematik Grundwissen 7. Klasse
Realschule Bayern .... Best.-Nr. 914057
Mathematik 8. Klasse
Realschule Bayern .... Best.-Nr. 91406
Mathematik 9. Klasse
Bayerischer Mathematiktest .... Best.-Nr. 91404
Funktionen 8.–10. Klasse
Realschule Bayern .... Best.-Nr. 91408
Lineare Gleichungssysteme .... Best.-Nr. 900122
Bruchzahlen und Dezimalbrüche .... Best.-Nr. 900061
Formelsammlung Mathematik
Realschule 5.–10. Klasse .... Best.-Nr. 51411
Kompakt-Wissen Realschule
Mathematik .... Best.-Nr. 914001
Übertritt in weiterführende Schulen .... Best.-Nr. 90002

Deutsch

Deutsch Grundwissen 5. Klasse
Realschule Bayern .... Best.-Nr. 91445
Deutsch Grundwissen 6. Klasse
Realschule Bayern .... Best.-Nr. 91446
Rechtschreibung und Diktat 5./6. Klasse   Best.-Nr. 90408
Nach den neuen Regeln, gültig ab 01.08.06.
Grammatik und Stil 7./8. Klasse .... Best.-Nr. 90407
Aufsatz 7./8. Klasse .... Best.-Nr. 91442
Aufsatz 9./10. Klasse
Realschule Baden-Württemberg .... Best.-Nr. 81440
Deutsch 9./10. Klasse Journalistische Texte
lesen, auswerten, schreiben .... Best.-Nr. 81442
Deutsche Rechtschreibung 5.–10. Klasse   Best.-Nr. 90402
Nach den neuen Regeln, gültig ab 01.08.06.
Text-Kompendien zum Kompetenzbereich
„Verstehen und Nutzen von Texten"
„Der olympische Gedanke –
und die Welt des Sports" .... Best.-Nr. 81443
„Demokratie leben heißt sich verantwortlich
fühlen und sich einmischen" .... Best.-Nr. 81444
„Jugendliche als Konsumenten zwischen
Beeinflussung und Selbstbestimmung" .. Best.-Nr. 81445
Kompakt-Wissen Realschule
Deutsch Aufsatz .... Best.-Nr. 514401
Kompakt-Wissen Rechtschreibung .... Best.-Nr. 944065
Nach den neuen Regeln, gültig ab 01.08.06.
Übertritt in weiterführende Schulen
mit CD .... Best.-Nr. 994402
Lexikon zur Kinder- und Jugendliteratur   Best.-Nr. 93443

Französisch

Französisch – Sprechsituationen und
Dolmetschen mit 2 CDs .... Best.-Nr. 91461
Rechtschreibung und Diktat
1./2. Lernjahr mit 2 CDs .... Best.-Nr. 905501
Wortschatzübung Mittelstufe .... Best.-Nr. 94510

Betriebswirtschaftslehre/Rechnungswesen

Betriebswirtschaftslehre/Rechnungswesen
Grundwissen 8. Klasse
Realschule Bayern .... Best.-Nr. 91473
Lösungsheft zu Best.-Nr. 91473 .... Best.-Nr. 91473L
Betriebswirtschaftslehre/Rechnungswesen
Grundwissen 9. Klasse
Realschule Bayern .... Best.-Nr. 91471
Lösungsheft zu Best.-Nr. 91471 .... Best.-Nr. 91471L
Betriebswirtschaftslehre/Rechnungswesen
Grundwissen 10. Klasse
Realschule Bayern .... Best.-Nr. 91472
Lösungsheft zu Best.-Nr. 91472 .... Best.-Nr. 91472L

Englisch

Englisch Grundwissen 5. Klasse .... Best.-Nr. 50505
Englisch – Hörverstehen 5. Klasse
mit CD .... Best.-Nr. 90512
Englisch – Rechtschreibung und Diktat
5. Klasse mit 3 CDs .... Best.-Nr. 90531
Englisch – Leseverstehen 5. Klasse .... Best.-Nr. 90526
Englisch – Wortschatzübung 5. Klasse
mit CD .... Best.-Nr. 90518
Englisch Grundwissen 6. Klasse .... Best.-Nr. 50506
Englisch – Hörverstehen 6. Klasse
mit CD .... Best.-Nr. 90511
Englisch – Rechtschreibung und Diktat
6. Klasse mit CD .... Best.-Nr. 90532
Englisch – Leseverstehen 6. Klasse .... Best.-Nr. 90525
Englisch – Wortschatzübung 6. Klasse
mit CD .... Best.-Nr. 90519
Englisch Grundwissen 7. Klasse .... Best.-Nr. 90507
Englisch – Hörverstehen 7. Klasse
mit CD .... Best.-Nr. 90513
Englisch Grundwissen 8. Klasse .... Best.-Nr. 90508
Englisch – Leseverstehen 8. Klasse .... Best.-Nr. 90522
Comprehension 1 / 8. Klasse .... Best.-Nr. 91453
Englisch Grundwissen 9. Klasse .... Best.-Nr. 90509
Englisch – Hörverstehen 9. Klasse
mit CD .... Best.-Nr. 90515
Englische Rechtschreibung 9./10. Klasse   Best.-Nr. 80453
Translation Practice 1 / ab 9. Klasse ...... Best.-Nr. 80451
Comprehension 2 / 9. Klasse .... Best.-Nr. 91452
Textproduktion 9./10. Klasse .... Best.-Nr. 90541
Englisch Grundwissen 10. Klasse .... Best.-Nr. 90510
Englisch – Hörverstehen 10. Klasse
mit CD .... Best.-Nr. 91457
Englisch – Leseverstehen 10. Klasse ...... Best.-Nr. 90521
Translation Practice 2 / ab 10. Klasse .... Best.-Nr. 80452
Comprehension 3 / 10. Klasse .... Best.-Nr. 91454
Systematische Vokabelsammlung .... Best.-Nr. 91455
Kompakt-Wissen Realschule
Englisch – Themenwortschatz .... Best.-Nr. 914501

Geschichte

Kompakt-Wissen Realschule
Geschichte .... Best.-Nr. 914801

Ratgeber für Schüler

Richtig Lernen
Tipps und Lernstrategien 5./6. Klasse
Schülerband: Äußere Arbeitsbedingungen; Anlaufschwierigkeiten beim Lernen; Arbeitseinteilung; Lernen und Gedächtnis; Lernrezepte für jeden Stoff; wie ich Zutrauen zu meinem Können fasse.
Elternband: Wie Sie Ihrem Kind helfen können; optimale Arbeitsbedingungen; typische Probleme bei den Hausaufgaben.
■ .... Best.-Nr. 10481

Richtig Lernen
Tipps und Lernstrategien 7. – 10. Klasse
Vermeidungsverhalten ab-, Motivation aufbauen; Arbeitseinteilung und Arbeitsorganisation; wie unser Gehirn Informationen auswählt und speichert; aus der Trickkiste der Gedächtniskünstler; Lernaufgaben erfolgreich meistern; das Können auf dem Prüfstand.
■ .... Best.-Nr. 10482

(Bitte blättern Sie um)

Bestellungen bitte direkt an:
STARK Verlag • Postfach 1852 • D-85318 Freising
Tel.: 08161/1790 • Fax: 08161/179-51 • www.stark-verlag.de • info@stark-verlag.de

Die echten Hilfen zum Lernen... **STARK**

Den Realschulabschluss erfolgreich meistern

- Vom Kultusministerium in Hamburg <u>zentral gestellte Prüfungsaufgaben für den Realschulabschluss</u>.

- Dazu ein <u>klar strukturierter Trainingsteil</u> und abwechslungsreiche <u>Übungsaufgaben</u> zu allen prüfungsrelevanten Kernkompetenzen.

- <u>Ausführliche, schülergerechte Lösungen</u> zu allen Aufgaben im integrierten, herausnehmbaren Lösungsheft.

- <u>Im übersichtlichen Format A4.</u>

- Ideal für Schülerinnen und Schüler <u>zur selbstständigen Vorbereitung auf die Abschlussprüfung</u>.

Mathematik

**Original-Prüfungsaufgaben
Mathematik
Realschulabschluss Hamburg**
Original-Prüfungsaufgaben 2005–2006: Dazu umfangreicher Trainingsteil und vermischte Übungsaufgaben. Zusätzlich wertvolle Hinweise zur Prüfung sowie eine Zusammenfassung aller wichtigen Begriffe, Lösungswege und Formeln. Im Format A4.
Ausführliche und schülergerechte Lösungen zu allen Aufgaben im integrierten, herausnehmbaren Lösungsheft.
■ .... Best.-Nr. 21500

Deutsch

**Original-Prüfungsaufgaben
Deutsch
Realschulabschluss Hamburg**
Original-Prüfungsaufgaben 2005–2006: Dazu umfassender Trainingsteil mit zahlreichen Übungen zu allen Aufgabenarten und Kernkompetenzen der Realschulabschluss-Prüfung in Hamburg. Enthält vielfältige Übungsaufgaben im Stil der Abschlussprüfung. Außerdem viele praktische Hinweise mit Beispielen und ein Überblick über das prüfungsrelevante Grundwissen. Format A4.
Ausführliche und schülergerechte Lösungen zu allen Aufgaben im herausnehmbaren Lösungsheft.
■ .... Best.-Nr. 21540

Englisch

**Original-Prüfungsaufgaben
Englisch mit CD
Realschulabschluss Hamburg**
Original-Prüfungsaufgaben 2005–2006: Dazu abwechslungsreiche Übungsaufgaben zur gezielten Vorbereitung auf die Realschulabschluss-Prüfung im Fach Englisch in Hamburg. Außerdem methodische Hilfen zum langfristigen, effektiven Lernen, systematische Wiederholung der englischen Grammatik und Hörverstehenstexte auf CD. Im Format A4.
Ausführliche und schülergerechte Lösungen zu allen Aufgaben mit hilfreichen Tipps im herausnehmbaren Lösungsheft.
■ .... Best.-Nr. 21550

Sämtliche Informationen zu unserem Gesamtprogramm finden Sie unter <u>www.stark-verlag.de</u>!

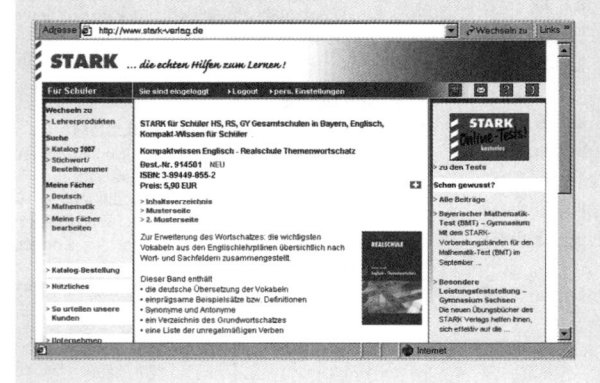

- Umfassende <u>Produktinformationen</u>
- Aussagekräftige <u>Musterseiten</u>
- <u>Inhaltsverzeichnisse</u> zu allen Produkten
- <u>Kostenlose Tests</u> im Internet für das Fach Mathematik. Ideal zum Aufdecken von Wissenslücken. Mit individueller Leistungsfeststellung und konkreten Vorschlägen zum Beheben der Lücken.
- Selbstverständlich können Sie auch im <u>Internet bestellen</u>

Bestellungen bitte direkt an:
STARK Verlag • Postfach 1852 • D-85318 Freising
Tel.: 08161/1790 • Fax: 08161/179-51 • www.stark-verlag.de • info@stark-verlag.de

Die echten Hilfen zum Lernen... **STARK**

REALSCHULE 2007

Original-Prüfungs-
aufgaben und Training

mit CD

Englisch

Realschulabschluss Hamburg
2005–2006

STARK

Bildnachweis
S. 19, S. 54, S. 70, S. 72–74, S. 77/78, S. 96/97: © Paul Jenkinson
S. 25: © www.sxc.hu
S. 34: © CorelDraw Inc.
S. 35: Foto 1: © Stephan Marti – visipix.com; Fotos 2, 5, 6: © www.sxc.hu; Foto 3: © www.celticnationsworld.com; Foto 4: © BilderBox.com
S. 45: © Dominic Arizona Bonuccelli
S. 2006-1: c) © stefaoz84/www.sxc.hu; Redaktion, d) © Redaktion; j) Sanja Gjenero/www.sxc.hu
S. 2006-6: Twelve Apostles: © Michael Chambers/www.sxc.hu; Dachzelt: © DAKTEC.de; Sydney Harbour Bridge: © Nicholas Rjabow/www.dreamstime.com; Uluru: © Steve Lovegrove/www.dreamstime.com; Kookaburra: © Vladimir Pomortsev/www.dreamstime.com; Dingo: © Jerry Dupree/www.dreamstime.com
Deckblatt Hinweise, Tipps und Übungsaufgaben zu den Kompetenzbereichen:
© Willselarep, Image provided by Dreamstime.com
Deckblatt Kurzgrammatik: © www.gimmestock.com/shakif
Deckblatt Original-Aufgaben der Abschlussprüfung an Realschulen in Hamburg: © James Moore

Umschlag: www.PixelQuelle.de

ISBN-13: 978-3-89449-825-2
ISBN-10: 3-89449-825-0

© 2006 by Stark Verlagsgesellschaft mbH & Co. KG
D-85318 Freising · Postfach 1852 · Tel. (0 81 61) 1790
2. ergänzte Auflage 2006
Nachdruck verboten!